EYEWITNESS EXPERT TESTIMONY

Handbook for the Forensic Psychiatrist, Psychologist and Attorney

Second Edition

EYEWITNESS EXPERT TESTIMONY

Handbook for the Forensic Psychiatrist, Psychologist and Attorney

R. Edward Geiselman, Ph.D.

For my daughter, Garianna, who has provided me with a lifetime of joy and happiness, and for my wife, Cynthia, who has given me Garianna, our second edition.

Copyright © 1994 ACFP Press
Second Edition Copyright © 1996 ACFP Press
All rights reserved.

ISBN 0-935645-00-4

No part of this book may be reproduced or transmitted in any form, including electronic, mechanical, photocopying, microfilming, recording, or otherwise, without written permission from the publisher.

ACFP Press
P.O. Box 5870
Balboa Island, California 92662

CONTENTS

Preface   5

1
Introduction   7

2
Basis for eyewitness expert testimony   13
- The *Amaral* decision
- Other appellant decisions

3
What eyewitness expert testimony can offer   25
- Importance of in-court questioning
- Expert as information seeker
- Examination of physical exhibits
- Expert's interviewing of eyewitnesses
- Special purpose experiments
- The expert's written report

4
Beginning a case   43

5
Current status of eyewitness research   49
- Laboratory studies
- Field studies

6
Current status of eyewitness expert testimony   57
- The issues
- The "battle of the experts"

7
Evaluation of eyewitness factors — 73
- The three stages of human information processing
- Taxonomy of eyewitness factors

8
Menu of direct examination questions — 121
- Establishing the expert's credentials
- The narrative on eyewitness information processing
- Substantive questions on eyewitness factors

9
Cross-examination questioning — 127

10
Preparing for re-direct questioning — 145

11
Courtroom demeanor of the expert — 149
- Message style
- Whom to address
- Body positioning and voice

12
Ethical dilemmas for psychologists as experts — 155
- Consultant-advocate distinction
- Contact from "the other side"
- Protecting the innocent versus freeing the guilty
- Accepting and declining cases

13
Alternatives to eyewitness expert testimony — 163
- Judge's model instructions to the jury
- Amicus curiae briefs
- Benefits and consequences of doing nothing

References — 171

Preface

This book is tailored to meet the needs of lawyers and social scientists who are interested in the prospect of applying forensic research on eyewitness performance in legal proceedings. With the recent federal and state Supreme Court rulings on expert evidence and the proper criteria for admissibility, it has become increasingly important that trial lawyers become sophisticated in the methods and procedures of science. The specific aim of this book is to provide a basis for enhancing the interaction between counsel and the eyewitness expert in the preparation of cases and the evaluation of eyewitness evidence under current procedures. Eyewitness psychologists have much to offer the legal system in a consulting role, yet the role of consultant is a delicate one given the adversary nature of litigation. Enhanced preparation can increase the likelihood that the impressive qualifications of an expert will translate into a "good witness" in court, both in terms of sound evidence and effective testimony.

For the past 22 years, I have participated as a basic and applied researcher, instructor, and consultant for law-enforcement agencies as well as for both the prosecution and defense in our adversary system. This experience hopefully has enabled me to frame the book to be of value to all involved. I have supported the key concepts throughout the book with selected case examples using scenarios from cases in which I was involved as an expert for the Superior Court of the County of Los Angeles, California.

The early chapters lay the foundation for expert testimony in eyewitness cases and explore what the testimony can offer the trier of fact. Subsequent chapters describe the current status of both eyewitness research and eyewitness expert testimony, including the fundamental issues in both areas as well as ethical dilemmas faced by psychologists who will serve as expert witnesses. In addition, a framework for evaluating the eyewitness evidence in a case is presented, which includes a taxonomy of factors that are most likely to affect eyewitness performance. Given that the quality of the expert testimony is in large part dependent on the quality of the questioning from the opposing counsels at trial, attention also is given to strategies for conducting direct, cross, and re-direct questioning of eyewitnesses experts. This book also may be of interest to those in the mental health profession as a general guide for offering expert testimony.

This second edition provides an up-to-date review of the research and issues in eyewitness psychology as of 1996, and provides additional laboratory and field evidence for the premises described in the first edition, as well as answers for additional questions.

1

Introduction

It has been estimated that each year approximately 77,000 individuals are arrested in the United States as suspects in cases where the principal evidence against the accused is testimony from eyewitnesses (Goldstein, Chance, & Schneller, 1989). Tollestrup, Turtle, and Yuille (1994) found that one out of five robbery cases in their sample resulted in a positive identification of a suspect by an eyewitness. The Rand Corporation (1975) concluded that the principal determinant of whether or not a case is solved is the completeness and accuracy of eyewitness accounts. Agents from law enforcement (Brigham & Wolfskeil, 1983; Sanders, 1986), the defense (Bailey & Rothblatt, 1985; Visher, 1987), and the courts (U.S. v. Wade, 1967) make similar claims about the importance of eyewitness testimony. Given the potential for eyewitness evidence to determine the outcome of a criminal case, it is critical that the testimony be obtained and evaluated carefully (Wall, 1965). In a study of 500 cases where a felony conviction was set aside because of clear and convincing new evidence, 60 percent of the cases hinged around eyewitness identifications (Huff, Rattner, & Sagarin, 1986). A similar result was obtained from a sample of 205 additional such cases (Rattner, 1988). In a 1986 survey of judges, prosecutors, and law-enforcement professionals, 8 out of 10 respondents concluded that, in their experience, witness error was the most common source of wrongful conviction

(Huff et al., 1986). Wells (1993) has documented 1,000 additional such cases since 1986. Even Thucydides (411 BC.), perhaps the first oral historian known, remarked that his history of the Peloponnesian War was laborious because the accounts of eyewitnesses to the same event varied so greatly.

A number of psycholegal approaches have been proposed in response to the problem of fallible eyewitness memory. Some social scientists have emphasized the value of early intervention during the investigations phase of the process. This intervention would take the form of better interview techniques for use by investigators to help eyewitnesses provide more complete and accurate reports (Fisher & Geiselman, 1992; Geiselman & Fisher, 1996), and better suspect identification procedures (Wells, 1988; Wells, Seelaw, Rydell, & Luus, 1994). Another "solution," often introduced by the prosecution and some law-enforcement personnel, is to deny the problem and do nothing. It follows from this conception that a unique and meaningful event such as an encounter with a criminal must have been etched permanently into the witness's memory, resulting in near-perfect recollection. Brigham and Wolfskeil (1983) found prosecutors and law-enforcement personnel in Florida to regard eyewitness identification as relatively accurate. It has been my experience, however, that most law-enforcement professionals readily acknowledge the problems and limitations of eyewitness reports, although they may not fully understand the factors involved (Yarmey, 1986). Likewise, an apparent motivation for the prosecution's position to deny the problem is to avoid the appearance of any doubt about the reliability of favorable eyewitnesses. In contrast, a lead prosecutor in a recent celebrated case in Los Angeles stated on at least three occasions that "circumstantial evidence is much more reliable than eyewitness evidence." She went on to say that "eyewitnesses are notoriously unreliable."

It was estimated in 1989 that eyewitness expert testimony was given as part of the defense case in 87% of the trials where it was admitted compared to only 13% for the prosecution, even though the experts said they would be willing to testify for either side (Kassin, Ellsworth, & Smith, 1989). This imbalance would be expected given that most eyewitnesses are called by the prosecution. There also is a different consideration for the appeals process with which the prosecution must contend. If an expert's testimony for the prosecution were to be viewed by a higher court as having been prejudicial, then the prosecution would run the risk of a guilty decision being overturned on appeal. Situations do arise, however, where eyewitness expert testimony would be advantageous for the prosecution's case, and there is some mock-trial evidence that with good eyewitnessing conditions, expert testimony can strengthen the prosecution's case (Cutler, Dexter, & Penrod, 1989). A colleague also related the following actual case in point. A victim of sexual assault positively identified her attacker and testified that his erect penis was extraordinarily large. The defense was prepared to call a number of other women who would testify from prior experience that the defendant's erect penis was among the smallest they had ever experienced. On this element of the evidence, the prosecution countered with an eyewitness expert who presented the results of psychological research showing that crime victims are prone to exaggerate key elements of the crime.

Some social scientists, while acknowledging the existence of the problem of fallible eyewitness recollection, concur that nothing is to be gained at present by a mixture of social scientists, counsels, judges, and juries in the courtroom (Egeth, 1995; Elliott, 1993; Konecni & Ebbesen, 1986; McKenna et al., 1992; McCloskey, Egeth, & McKenna, 1986). This position has been debated in the social science literature and many of the issues involved are discussed in Chapter 6. In contrast, legal scholar and social scientist Hugo Munsterberg acknowledged the fallibility of eyewitness testimony at the turn of the century. He advanced the argument that "experimental psychology has reached a stage at which it seems natural and sound to give attention also to its possible service for the practical needs of life" (from "On the witness stand," 1908, p. 8). He further stated that "while the court makes fullest use of all the modern scientific methods when...a drop of dried blood is to be examined...the same court is completely satisfied with...common prejudice and ignorance when a mental product, especially the memory report of a witness, is to be examined" (p. 45). In several mock-trial simulation studies, jurors have been found by as much as two to one to believe in the accuracy of eyewitnesses who made false identifications (Lindsay, Wells, & Rumpel, 1981). Psychology has just celebrated the one-hundred and sixteenth anniversary of the founding of the first recognized laboratory for psychological research at Leipzig, Germany, in 1879. The American Psychological Association currently publishes approximately 20 scholarly journals containing thousands of formal experiments. Interest in the psychology of eyewitness testimony flourished at the turn of the last century with the work of such notable social scientists as Munsterberg. Forensic eyewitness psychology enjoyed a revival of sorts in the 1970s (Loftus, 1979; Wells, 1978; Yarmey, 1979), continuing to the present (Cutler & Penrod, 1995; Ross, Read, & Toglia, 1994; Williams, Loftus, & Deffenbacher, 1992), with an entire division of the American Psychological Association now devoted to the domain of Psychology and Law (Division 41). It has been claimed that "research on evidence produced by eyewitnesses to an event is among the most systematic and theoretically developed in the psychology of law" (Monahan & Loftus, 1982, p. 450). One eyewitness psychologist has amassed a bibliography of over 2,000 references (Penrod, Fulero, & Cutler, 1995), while another cited 120 studies published between 1980 and 1992 (Williams et al., 1992). Thus, the foundation has been laid for the use of eyewitness expert testimony to assist the trier of fact in a court of law. By 1988, some 450 trials in 25 states had admitted expert testimony on eyewitness evidence (Brigham, 1988). With increasing frequency during the past decade, social scientists have presented their findings on eyewitness matters as expert witnesses in criminal and civil cases (Penrod et al., 1995). The legal basis for the admission of eyewitness expert testimony is presented in Chapter 2.

The purpose for eyewitness expert testimony is to assist a judge or jury in more fully understanding the capabilities and limitations of eyewitnesses. In doing so, the expert relies on the research literature from eyewitness psychology to describe factors that are generally believed to reliably affect the performance of a significant percentage of eyewitnesses. The purpose for this book is to provide information from a variety of perspectives to facilitate the attorney/expert collaborative effort in carrying out this mission. Based on my experience as a researcher, instructor, and consultant on eyewitness matters, I believe that judges and juries would be better served by a population of counsels and potential eyewitness experts who are more fully informed about the issues most typically entertained during direct, cross, and re-direct examination in court. One lawyer and legal scholar has noted that the rigorous scrutiny of eyewitness expert testimony is going to demand "a sophistication of scientific understanding for which few are currently equipped. Many lawyers will be on a sharp learning curve" (Freckelton, 1993). Thus, this book addresses case preparation and testimony on behalf of both the prosecution (plaintiff) and defense, as well as preparation for cross and re-direct examination from either side.

2

Basis for Eyewitness Expert Testimony

In 1975, Rule 702 of the United States Federal Rules of Evidence was enacted as follows: "If scientific, technical, or other specialized knowledge will assist the trier of fact to understand the evidence or to determine a fact in issue, a witness qualified as an expert by knowledge, skill, experience, training, or education, may testify thereto in the form of an opinion or otherwise."

The Federal Rules of Evidence often serve as models for the state and local courts in the adoption of similar, if not identical statutes. It would appear, then, that expert testimony from social scientists on factors affecting eyewitness performance would be readily admitted by trial courts. However, under the traditional evidentiary standards requiring testimony be based on first-hand knowledge of the evidence, the expert's opinion testimony is the exception rather than the rule. As such, the proponent of the expert testimony bears the burden of persuading a court of its value and necessity to gain admission of the testimony.

The *Amaral* Decision

Perhaps the leading legal opinion concerning eyewitness expert testimony was rendered by the Ninth Circuit Court of

Appeals in *U.S. v. Amaral* (1973). While upholding the lower court's ruling to exclude eyewitness expert testimony in the case, the appellate court held that in order to be admissible, any scientific expert testimony must satisfy the following four criteria:

(1) The witness must be a qualified expert. In practice, this criterion is met in the wisdom of most courts if the proposed expert holds the Ph.D. degree, has taught courses related to eyewitness issues, has conducted research on some aspect of eyewitness performance, has published the findings of the research, and perhaps has qualified as an expert on prior occasions. It has been my observation, however, that a Ph.D. degree in a relevant discipline from a reputable institution of higher learning often will suffice in some courts.

(2) The testimony must concern a proper subject matter. This criterion has been interpreted in terms of two overlapping standards. First, the testimony must be based on such specialized knowledge as to be beyond the experience and understanding of the average layperson. Early court decisions declared that the subjects of perception and memory were sufficiently within the expertise of the jury, and their common-sense knowledge would enable them to evaluate the likelihood of a mistaken identification without the assistance of an expert. The opinion in *People v. Guzman* (1975) read: "It is something everyone knows about, the problems of identification."

Loftus (1986) noted in her memoirs after the first 10 years as an expert witness that her testimony was frequently ruled inadmissible on these grounds. Recently, however, some appellate courts have recognized that the body of literature on eyewitness testimony is beyond the common experience of the average juror (*People v. McDonald*, 1984; *State v. Chapple*, 1983; *State v. Moon*, 1986). In agreement with these rulings, published survey research suggests that certain key eyewitness factors are not fully understood by a significant percentage of laypersons (Brigham & Bothwell, 1983; Deffenbacher & Loftus, 1982; Kassin & Barndollar, 1992; Lindsay, 1994; Loftus, 1979; Ramirez, Zemba, & Geiselman, 1996; Saks & Hastie, 1978). For instance, laypersons appear not to understand the potential negative consequences of cross-racial identification nor that eyewitness confidence is not necessarily a good indicator of eyewitness accuracy. Based a series of recent studies with persons eligible for jury duty, Lindsay (1994) concluded that "expert testimony on eyewitness issues easily meets the legal criteria of admissibility; most people have little idea of how to evaluate the accuracy of an eyewitness identification, underestimate the importance of many relevant variables, and apply significantly wrong expectations regarding other variables" (p. 381).

The second interpretation of the "proper subject matter" criterion precludes experts from testifying if their testimony would usurp the jury's function as the trier of fact to decide the credibility of witnesses (*U.S. v. Brown*, 1976). However, as will become apparent in the chapters that follow, the eyewitness expert avoids giving an expert opinion as to the reliability of any particular eyewitness in the case at hand. Instead, the expert testimony addresses the processes of observing, remembering and recalling memories, while attempting to dispel common misconceptions concerning those processes and to describe factors that would likely affect the reliability of eyewitness identifications. Thus, as a general justification for excluding eyewitness expert testimony, this objection currently is being rejected in the majority of jurisdictions.

(3) **The testimony must be in accordance with a generally accepted explanatory theory.** This criterion was established in *People v. Frye* (1923) with regard to the admissibility of polygraph evidence and also has been applied to the forensic use of hypnosis (*People v. Shirley*, 1982). Expert testimony must be based upon a theory sufficiently established to have gained general acceptance in its field. Meeting this criterion is especially difficult for the discipline of psychology where alternative conceptions of the same data and debates over the appropriate design and interpretation of experiments are easily found. One prominent cognitive psychologist lamented in 1981 that "I have studied memory for years, yet am unable to answer even simple questions about the use of memory in everyday life" (Norman, 1981, p. 271).

Specific to eyewitness expert testimony, one trial court ruled in 1975 that "there is no generally recognized area of research on the subject of eyewitness identification" *(U.S. v. Jackson*, 1975). Similarly, one judge rejected the testimony of an eyewitness expert "because as a scientific field, eyewitness identification has not been sufficiently established to have gained general acceptance within the field of psychology as a whole" (Sobel, 1972, p. 62). There is some debate among experimental psychologists themselves on this issue, and the debate is discussed in Chapter 6.

However, a survey of experts on eyewitness testimony published not long ago in the American Psychological Association journal *The American Psychologist* revealed a strong consensus (as much as 70-85%) that certain psychological findings are sufficiently well established and could profitably be described to a jury (Kassin et al., 1989). Other published surveys further suggest that there is general agreement among social scientists who would qualify as eyewitness identification experts as to major findings and interpretations in the field of witness psychology (Kassin & Barndollar, 1992; Yarmey & Jones, 1983). In concordance with the apparent maturation of the field, more recent court rulings have been more favorable toward admitting eyewitness expert testimony. In *U.S. v. Smith* (1984), the court concluded that "the day may have arrived, therefore, when [the expert's] testimony can be said to conform to a generally accepted explanatory theory."

Furthermore, the generally accepted theory requirement has been challenged successfully in both Federal Courts (e.g., *U.S. v. Downing*, 1985) and in a recent U.S. Supreme Court ruling (*Daubert v. Merrell Dow Pharmaceuticals, Inc.*, 1993). *Daubert* involved proffered expert testimony on whether an antinausea drug caused birth defects. The Supreme Court found that "a rigid 'general acceptance' requirement would be at odds with the 'liberal thrust' of the Federal Rules of Evidence and their general approach of relaxing the traditional barriers to 'opinion' testimony." Instead, the court ruled that to be admissible as expert evidence, it must be scientific, which "...implies a grounding in the methods and procedures of science..." It must be "...more than subjective belief or unsupported speculation." It also "...must be supported by appropriate validation..." With this decision, judges will have to be satisfied not just of the predominant view within the relevant scientific field but also of the integrity of the research upon which the expert testimony is based. With *Daubert*, the emphasis clearly has shifted from findings to methods. Another important consideration from *Daubert* is whether the theory or technique has been subjected to peer review and publication. It is therefore imperative that judges, counsels, and legal scholars be aware of the relevant issues and literature presented in Chapters 5, 6, 7, and 8, especially those working within the federal courts.

For further explication of the *Daubert* ruling, see Black & Singer (1993), Melton (1995), Penrod et al. (1995), and Underwager & Wakefield (1993). At the time of this publication, well over 100 articles had been written on the anticipated impact of the *Daubert* ruling, but only a few state courts had adopted the Daubert criteria, with most holding to the rule. The State Supreme Court of California, for example, rejected the Daubert rule in favor of Kelley, which is that state's version of the Frye rule (*People v. Leahy,* 1994).

(4) The probative value of the testimony must outweigh its prejudicial effects. This criterion permits the trial judge to exclude testimony that would undermine the truth-finding process or interfere with the administration of justice, and is usually invoked in combination with one of the other criteria for the admission of expert testimony (Woocher, 1986). Historically, this criterion has been cited to avoid needless expenditure of time and money required to introduce the testimony of the eyewitness expert. A prime example is where the evidence corroborating the identity of the person in question is sufficiently clear such that the expert testimony would add little to the proceedings (see *U.S. v. Collins,* 1975). In such situations, the court must consider the possibility that the expert's credentials might lead the jury to rely too heavily on the opinion of the expert and undervalue the weight of other evidence. At the federal level,

Daubert did not alter the district courts' discretionary power to exclude expert testimony "if its probative value is substantially outweighed by the danger of unfair prejudice, confusion of the issues, or misleading the jury."

One legal expert and social scientist has concluded that "if [judges] think the prosecution's case is weak, they tend to allow the expert testimony, and if they think the prosecution's case is strong, they tend to exclude it" (Lempert, 1986, p. 171). The same rationale would apply to the admission of eyewitness expert testimony on behalf of the prosecution, and his contention is well supported by the often cited decision of the California Supreme Court in *People v. McDonald* (1984): "When an eyewitness identification of the defendant is a key element of the prosecution's case *but is not substantially corroborated by evidence giving it independent reliability* (my italics), and the defendant offers qualified expert testimony on specific psychological factors shown by the record that could have affected the accuracy of the identification but are not likely to be fully known to or understood by the jury, it will ordinarily be error to exclude that testimony."

Other Appellant Decisions

The first appellate court decision in which it was ruled that a trial judge abused his discretion when he barred an eyewitness expert from testifying appears to have been based more on a the questionable honesty of the "eyewitnesses" in the case than on the traditional issues of reliability raised in eyewitness expert testimony. In the often cited matter of *State v. Chapple* (1983), the "eyewitnesses" (accusers) were co-participants in a homicide and had been together with the perpetrator in question for several days in a series of activities such as riding in a car and drinking. Thus, the identity of the defendant should not have been a significant issue in the case. The defendant, however, had a credible alibi and the "eyewitnesses" stood to benefit from a plea bargain to identify someone. It was perhaps this mixture of evidence and circumstances that led Judge Hayes to explain his dissenting opinion in the case as follows: "My concern here goes beyond the borders of this case. Once we have opened the door to this sort of impeaching testimony, what is to prevent experts from attacking any real or supposed deficiency in every other mental faculty? ...I have great reluctance to permit academia to take over the fact-finding function of the jury. Although clothed in other guise, that will be the practical effect." Judge Hayes appears to have seen the coming of Alan Dershowitz's *The Abuse Excuse* (1994). Nevertheless, the court's majority ruling in the *Chapple* case established a precedent for the admission of eyewitness expert testimony that other appellate courts had previously refused to endorse. Several additional states have admitted eyewitness expert testimony since *Chapple*, including Alaska (*Skamarocius v. State*, 1987), New York (*People v. Lewis*, 1987), Ohio (*State v. Buell*, 1986), and Florida (*State v. Malarney*, 1993). For a more comprehensive review of such case law, see Cutler and Penrod (1995). There are comparable precedent cases to permit eyewitness expert testimony in juvenile courts.

The admission of eyewitness expert testimony has not gone unchallenged since *Chapple*, however, and one trial court's exclusion of expert testimony was upheld on appeal in a recent case in California (*U.S. v. Rincon*, 1993). The United

States Court of Appeals for the Ninth Circuit ruled that the testimony was properly excluded in that it did not meet two of the four criteria established in *Amaral*. With respect to the "generally accepted theory" criterion, the court's opinion read: "Psychologists do not generally accept the claimed dangers of eyewitness identification in a trial setting." Citing a paper by McCloskey and Egeth (1983), the opinion read: "There is virtually no empirical evidence that [jurors] are unaware of the problems with eyewitness testimony." However, the court's ruling appeared to reflect weaknesses in Rincon's arguments at the district court level more than weaknesses in the current state of the "generally accepted theory criterion." The opinion reads: "Rincon's counsel... only cited a few state and federal courts in support of that proposition, none of which control here. While we are aware that other federal courts and state courts are beginning to accept expert testimony on the psychological factors affecting eyewitness identifications, the reasoning behind those authorities is better directed to the district court at the time it exercises its discretion."

With respect to the "probative value" criterion, the appeals court dismissed Rincon's offer of proof and concluded that "the effects of stress, cross-gender or cross-ethnic identifications, suggestibility, and passage of time were not beyond the bounds of the jurors' common knowledge." There is considerable debate concerning the veracity of this assertion (see Chapter 6) and survey evidence contrary to the court's opinion is cited throughout this book. The opinion of the court further stated that "cross-examination was sufficient to reveal any deficiencies in the eyewitness testimony." This assertion is consistent with the court's desire to minimize unnecessary expenditures of time and resources, and it has been re-affirmed at the California state court level *(People v. Gaglione*, 1994). While there is some evidence from mock-trial experiments in support of the court's opinion (Kennedy & Haygood, 1992), most of the evidence casts doubt on the effectiveness of cross-examination with confident witnesses (Lindsay, Wells, & O'Connor, 1989; Wells, Lindsay, & Ferguson, 1979). Finally, the opinion read: "The district court judge instructed the jury as to the potential unreliability of eyewitness testimony, that innocent miss-recollection, like failure of recollection, is not an uncommon experience." The use of judge's instructions as an alternative to eyewitness expert testimony has been tried in some *jurisdictions (U.S. v. Telfaire*, 1972), but there is considerable empirical evidence that these instructions are ineffective, and perhaps even prejudicial, in their present form. The impact of judge's instructions on jury decision making is discussed in Chapter 13.

The exclusionary ruling in the *Rincon* matter reaffirms that "the trial court has 'broad discretion' to admit or exclude expert testimony...and [the appeals court] will not reverse the trial court's ruling unless [the appeals court] concludes that it was manifestly erroneous" (*U.S. v. Poole*, 1986). As a result of a post-*Daubert* appeal, the Ninth Circuit revisited the *Rincon* matter and upheld the earlier decision (*U.S. v. Rincon*, 1994). In contrast, the Third Circuit appellate court has been more receptive to eyewitness expert testimony (e.g., *U.S. v. Downing*, 1985; *U.S. v. Stevens*, 1991). Penrod et al. (1995) anticipate that the appellate courts will become more uniformly in support of eyewitness expert testimony as the *Daubert* ruling takes hold.

In practice, the discretion to exclude eyewitness expert testimony altogether is currently more likely in jurisdictions where the option to present expert testimony has not been exercised with any regularity. Even this pattern is not without exception, however. In *People v. Brandon* (1995), the presiding trial judge denied a defense motion to exclude an eyewitness identification based on the results of a "special purpose experiment" conducted on the photoarray by an eyewitness expert (not the author). The experiment had been conducted to assess the fairness of the photoarray. Such judicial denials are common and there is some debate as to whether it is ethical for experts to present the results of special purpose experiments as testimony (see Chapter 3). Nevertheless, this judge's ruling on the exclusionary motion and similar rulings have been interpreted liberally by other judges to exclude an expert from giving opinion testimony about the biased nature of a specific photoarray during trial.

At least one trial judge in Los Angeles has taken the exclusionary process even one step further by denying an expert from mentioning any element of the facts of the case in his testimony. Relying on *People v. Sandoval* (1994), the judge ruled that it was the province of the jury to decide whether a particular photoarray was biased. Thus, the standard limitation on an expert to refrain from speaking to the ultimate issue of a defendant's guilt or to the accuracy of a particular eyewitness's identification has been extended to an evaluation of the physical exhibits used in a case. Rulings such as these appear contrary to what sets experts apart from other witnesses; experts generally are allowed to go beyond the facts and give opinions. Some eyewitness experts agree with these court rulings, however, in that the ultimate judgment of lineup fairness should be left to the trier of fact (Wells, Leippe, & Ostrom, 1979). Even these scholars, however, firmly believe that the courts must be cognizant of the conceptual underpinnings and empirical characteristics of lineup fairness measures. Expert testimony is needed to describe to the trier of fact the known effects of biased lineups on eyewitness identification performance and how lineup fairness is evaluated by researchers in eyewitness psychology.

In light of the variety of recent exclusionary rulings, counsels and experts must be prepared prior to trial for a range of last minute limitations on the testimony. Alternative sets of questions and answers should be considered that present the eyewitness factors relevant to the case (see Chapters 7) without explicitly addressing the elements of the case. The expert can review the literature on the relevant eyewitness factors using general questions such as those presented in Chapter 8, with the counsel tying those factors to the elements of the case during closing argument. It is my understanding that the recent exclusionary rulings are still an exception to general judicial practice concerning eyewitness expert testimony, but they are becoming increasingly more common.

3

What Eyewitness Expert Testimony Can Offer

Eyewitness expert testimony can assist the judge or jury in more fully understanding the capabilities and limitations of eyewitnesses. Testimony is offered in the context of factors that are generally believed to reliably affect the recollections of a significant percentage of eyewitnesses. As noted in Chapter 2, there are several dimensions of eyewitness performance where the beliefs of judges and laypersons are not necessarily consistent with the conclusions drawn from research by social scientists who qualify as eyewitness experts. With input from recognized experts in the field, doubt held by a judge or a juror concerning the reliability of testimony by an eyewitness can be converted into a more fully informed doubt. There is evidence from mock trial experiments indicating an increase in juror perceived credibility of an eyewitness with supportive expert testimony and a decrease in perceived credibility with unsupportive expert testimony (Blonstein & Geiselman, 1990).

The testimony that an expert may offer either in a pre-trial report or at trial includes a discussion of factors that are generally believed to reliably affect a significant percentage of eyewitnesses. The expert can review relevant scientific research on the ability to perceive and recall complex events and can set out various cognitive and social factors that are known to reliably distort or enhance perception, hamper or maintain memory, and alter or facilitate recollection. A taxonomy of these factors is presented in Chapter 7 and alternative formats for presenting the factors at trial is offered in Chapter 8. While the effects of some of these factors will seem obvious upon first consideration, surveys of laypersons suggest otherwise (see Chapter 6). Fischhoff (1975) has found evidence that people can have opposite beliefs and find either one to be obvious after the fact in hindsight. Even when the effects are known to jurors, many have remarked at the end of a trial in which I have appeared that "it was good to hear it from an expert so that I could act on what I believed to be true about the eyewitness's testimony." As an example, Wells (1984) speculates that some jurors might argue in deliberations that the saying "They all look alike to me" is a racist myth without any scientific merit. He further speculates that "social desirability considerations may prevent the jurors from openly discussing the issue at all for fear that it would be perceived as racially biased. It seems safer to have the issue clearly aired by an expert to ensure that the cross-race factor is considered."

An expert cannot express an opinion that the eyewitness testimony of any particular person is reliable or unreliable, nor can the expert generally testify as to whether any particular piece of testimony is accurate. Melton (1995) notes that "even if there is no harm in admitting ultimate-issue opinions, psychologists are ethically bound not to offer them" (p. 65). Instead, the expert's role is to inform the judge or jury about the processes of observing, remembering, and recalling memories, to dispel common misconceptions concerning those processes, and to discuss factors that would likely affect the reliability of eyewitness identifications. Thus, eyewitness expert testimony is of a probabilistic nature about factors that are generally believed to reliably affect a significant percentage of eyewitnesses rather than about the accuracy of recollections by any particular eyewitness. It should be noted that the eyewitnesses themselves also are giving only probabilistic information about what the believe they remember (Wells, 1984), and they are not precluded from testifying based on this limitation.

Historically, some courts have struggled with the distinction between the function of eyewitness experts and the frequent function of mental health or psychiatric experts to render opinions on state of mind, competency, or the legal sanity of a particular person. In *People v. Johnson* (1974), which preceded McDonald by ten years, a California court used its discretion to disallow eyewitness expert testimony because "psychiatric testimony cannot be used to impeach a witness in cases not involving sex offenses" (Penrod et al., 1995). Contrary to this decision, the role of the eyewitness expert is neither to provide psychiatric testimony nor to impeach a particular witness as being inaccurate.

Importance of In-Court Questioning

The quality of the testimony ultimately depends in large part on the quality of the questions that are asked of the expert. The expert testimony is framed foremost in questions asked by counsel during direct examination. As much as possible, the expert must play an integral role in formulating the direct examination questions. Most experts offer the retaining counsel a menu of potential questions in advance of trial that are relevant to the case at hand. A suggested set of such questions is presented in Chapter 8. It is especially important for the retaining counsel to discuss any hypothetical questions that will be put to the expert in advance of trial. Confusion over the intended meaning of these questions can be extremely disruptive.

The initial questions typically elicit a narrative overview on the nature of eyewitness perception, memory, and recollection followed by substantive questions about the literature concerning specific eyewitness factors such as stress, confidence, and race, as they relate to eyewitness accuracy. The expert presents relevant laboratory and field research from the literature in support of the expert opinion. Ethical guidelines of the American Psychological Association (1981) and recommendations from the courts (Bazelon, 1982) require psychologists to also provide a discussion of the limitations of the data from which they draw their expert opinions. This discussion usually addresses the general strengths and weaknesses of laboratory and field experiments on direct examination and becomes more specific on cross-examination with respect to the specific experiments cited by the expert.

The expert testimony typically is presented at a conceptual level with the counsel linking the factors discussed by the expert explicitly to the facts in the case during closing arguments. One exception to this rule is the expert's evaluation of any physical exhibits in the case such as a photoarray used to identify the defendant. Some counsels also may elect to pose hypothetical questions to the expert to summarize the expert's testimony in the context of the facts of the case at hand.

The importance of the quality of direct examination questioning has led me to be reluctant to accept *Propria-Persona* cases, where the defendant has been granted the option of serving as his own counsel. While I respect a defendant's option to serve as his own attorney, my experience in a handful of these cases has been frustrating at best. Even though I provide each of these "Pro Per" defendants with a menu of direct examination questions, they routinely deviate from the questioning format in unexpected and sometimes illogical ways, with the opposing counsel objecting throughout. Under such nearly chaotic conditions, I have felt that the expert testimony was entirely ineffective.

Of course, the effectiveness of the expert testimony also depends on the questioning by the opposing counsel during cross-examination. Given that the strategy of the opposing counsel is only somewhat predictable, the trial experience of the eyewitness expert is important. The arguments that an eyewitness expert faces most frequently on cross-examination are discussed in Chapter 9. Each of these arguments can be addressed by the expert during either cross or re-direct questioning. In most cases, however, the expert does not have the opportunity to consult with counsel after cross-examination to formulate questioning for re-direct examination. It therefore is imperative that general plans for re-direct questioning be discussed in advance of the expert's appearance at trial. In this manner, the arguments previously brought out on direct examination can be reinforced, elaborated, and clarified. Some strategies for advance preparation of re-direct questioning are presented in Chapter 10.

Expert as Information Seeker

The quality of the expert's testimony also is contingent upon the expert having access to an accurate and complete description of the eyewitness evidence in the case from the outset. Pursuant to this end, part of the expert's role as consultant is to confer with counsel on questions raised by the expert's examination of the evidence contained in the police, investigator, and court documents. For example, I have participated in several cases where the investigator's reports indicated that the eyewitnesses made "positive" identifications of the defendant. Upon obtaining copies of the witness admonishment forms at my request, however, many of these witnesses had written that they selected the person who "most closely resembled" their recollection of the perpetrator. While these statements are somewhat diagnostic in considering the totality of eyewitness evidence, a relative judgment is not the same thing as a positive identification. Tollestrup et al. (1994) have reported similar instances from their field study of actual cases of robbery. There is evidence that witnesses who make relative judgments are less likely to be accurate than witnesses who make positive identifications (Stern & Dunning, 1994).

In one specific case, the investigator's report and preliminary hearing transcript described two positive identifications of a defendant by bank tellers. I found it odd that only two persons in a crowded bank had been asked to make an identification. Further inquiries at my request revealed that ten other witnesses who were not mentioned in the documents either selected someone else from the photoarray or stated that the robber was not present in the array. The totality of eyewitness evidence formed a picture that was quite different from the original subset of the evidence. The existence of nonidentification evidence impacts the evaluation of any positive identifications of the defendant and nonidentifications also are properly interpreted as a form of exonerating evidence (Wells & Lindsay, 1980).

The expert should not restrict the evaluation of evidence to information contained in the documents supplied initially by counsel. Instead, the expert can contribute valuable insights during the evaluation toward a more complete and accurate assessment of the eyewitness evidence. Wells (1984) notes that "anyone who gets calls from attorneys asking for expert testimony realizes how many factors they do overlook" (p. 309). The contribution of the expert as an information seeker need not lead the expert to stray from the role of consultant and into the domain of the advocate. The information is sought to maximize the completeness and accuracy of the knowledge base upon which the expert opinion is derived, and its effect is not necessarily to enhance the strength of the client's case over that of the other. In this regard, the *Specialty Guidelines for Forensic Psychologists* (American Psychological Association, 1991) states that an expert should "actively seek information that will differentially test plausible rival hypotheses." I routinely pose questions to counsels that might appear as challenges to their adversary position on the eyewitness evidence.

Examination of Physical Exhibits

A major exception to the rule that an expert's in-court testimony should be limited to general cognitive and social factors is the evaluation of physical exhibits, principally photoarrays and police photos of live lineups submitted in the case. Numerous published research studies have addressed the potentially biasing effects of procedures by which some photoarrays and live lineups are constructed (see Chapter 7). The biasing effects are sometimes quite obvious, such as a black defendant being placed in a photoarray with five Caucasian alternatives. Instances of blatant departures from standard police procedures have been documented (Lindsay, 1994; Loftus, 1979). In other cases, the biasing effects are more subtle and are tied to the facts of the particular case. In these instances, testimony from an expert may be warranted to bolster the credibility of the counsel's argument. For example, I was asked to examine a photoarray where all of the persons depicted had brown eyes except for one who had green eyes. This would appear irrelevant except that the perpetrator in the case was said to have sounded like a gang member with the moniker "green eyes." A bystander heard this comment and later selected the suspect's photo from the biased array.

In a case from another state, a photo of a live lineup revealed one person holding an unlit cigarette between two fingers at his side. Again, this fact would appear irrelevant were it not for the fact that the suspect in this matter was said to have reeked of cigarette smoke at the crime scene. In yet another case, an experienced detective testified that he had attempted to make sure that none of the persons in the array he constructed appeared similar. This was so that no one person would stand out from the rest. He further testified that he thought that he had achieved his objective. It was my opinion that he had achieved his goal such that only the suspect in the case fit the verbal description given by the lone witness. Thus, the photoarray probably had a functional size of only one alternative for the witness to choose from.

In each of these cases, the eyewitness identification evidence potentially was tainted as a result of biasing factors that could be addressed by an expert, either in a written report or in trial testimony. Expert testimony in the form of a written report can be used in a pre-trial motion by either the defense or prosecution to suppress eyewitness identification evidence unfavorable to their side. In each of the cases cited here, pre-trial motions by the defense to suppress were denied. Such denials are common and there have been many other decisions by trial judges to deny the suppression of identifications that were obtained with seemingly biased procedures. Lindsay (1994) has concluded from survey research that unfair lineup procedures are poorly understood by judges. In *People v. Holt* (1982), the defendant's picture appeared in color whereas the others were black and white. In *People v. Blair* (1979), the defendant was seven years older and 37 pounds heavier than any other person in the lineup. In *People v. Faulkner* (1972), the defendant was shortest by five inches. In *People v. Thomas* (1970), the defendant was the only person barefoot. In *People v. Perkins* (1986), an officer at the lineup informed the witness that the defendant has specific tattoos that the witness had reported earlier.

These rulings usually are not taken further to preclude an expert from discussing the potentially biased aspects of an array at trial. In fact, in each of the above case examples where I participated, my expert testimony about the arrays was cited by the trier of fact as a basis for a not guilty decision. In cases such as these, the prosecution has the option to call an eyewitness expert to bolster the contention of fairness of the photoarray or live lineup.

In a separate case, the judge did grant a motion by the opposing counsel to exclude my expert testimony at trial concerning potentially biased aspects of a specific photoarray that had been admitted as a physical exhibit. In that case, the photo of the defendant was extremely overexposed and both eyewitnesses in the case had emphasized the light complexion of the suspect in their reports to the police. The defendant in fact had rather dark skin. I had discussed this potentially biasing aspect of the photoarray with the defense counsel who was prepared to ask me to comment on the fairness of the array at trial during direct examination. However, with the explicit exclusion of such testimony by the judge immediately prior to my appearance, my testimony was limited to general factors and issues of fairness in photoarray construction. The defense counsel then successfully linked my testimony with the potentially biased nature of the photoarray during closing arguments. Both counsel and expert must be prepared for such rulings in advance of the expert's appearance with an alternative set of questions for direct examination that will present the relevant issues of photoarray or lineup fairness without explicitly referring to the particular exhibits in the case.

Expert's Interviewing of Eyewitnesses

The task of the trier of fact, be it the judge or the jury, is to evaluate the credibility of specific eyewitnesses rather than "the typical eyewitness." As a result, many if not most jurors probably wonder why the expert would not interview the eyewitnesses in the case before them. In fact, this question is routinely asked of eyewitness experts during cross-examination by the opposing counsel in an attempt to discredit the relevance of the expert testimony (see Chapter 9). In most cases, however, little if anything useful can be learned from an in-person examination of eyewitnesses by an eyewitness expert. This is especially true with the usually significant time lag before an expert is appointed to the case. Scientific research has produced little in the way of witness characteristics that can predict who is likely to be a good witness, and even less about who would be most prepared psychologically to perceive and remember well under the specific conditions at hand (see Chapter 7). Even if psychologists were to devise a test to evaluate a person's "eyewitness ability," that tool would most assuredly come under great legal scrutiny, as it should.

Therefore, there is rarely anything to be gained from an in-person examination of an eyewitness by an eyewitness expert beyond that which can be obtained from a careful examination of the police reports, investigator reports, and other court documents. This sets eyewitness expert testimony apart from other psychological evaluations, such as child custody evaluations, in that the subjects must be interviewed to provide an expert opinion in these other domains except in limited cases (see guidelines in the July, 1994, issue of American Psychologist). An in-person examination of the clinical state of an eyewitness by a qualified mental health professional may be relevant as to the cognitive functioning of the witness, but this is another matter. Should an eyewitness expert elect not interview the eyewitness, the *Specialty Guidelines for Forensic Psychologists* (American Psychological Association, 1991) is quite clear in that "forensic psychologists [should] avoid giving written or oral evidence about the psychological characteristics of particular individuals when they have not had an opportunity to conduct an examination of the individual adequate to the scope of the statements, opinions, or conclusions to be issued."

Special Purpose Experiments

It is tempting for the eyewitness expert to stage an experiment to evaluate his/her conclusions about the eyewitness evidence. If a photoarray or lineup appears to be biased in some fashion, an experiment could be designed to test the exhibit for fairness. This could be done by showing the exhibit to persons not familiar with the case and asking them to guess the suspect based only on the verbal descriptions given by the actual eyewitnesses. If the defendant were selected by significantly more of the naive persons than would be expected by them simply guessing, then the array or lineup would be said to be biased. With a six-person array or lineup, one-sixth of the naive persons should select the suspect by guessing. Social scientists often use this and similar procedures to evaluate photoarrays for fairness in laboratory research (Brigham & Pfeifer, 1994; Doob & Kirshenbaum, 1973; Wells, 1993). It is a different situation, however, when such tests are carried out on photoarrays or lineups from actual cases for the explicit purpose of presenting the results at trial. Most social scientists who provide eyewitness expert testimony consider such a practice to be extremely dangerous, if not unethical (Konecni & Ebbesen, 1986; Loftus, 1986).

First, there would be no guarantee that the impromptu experiment would itself be designed fairly, and it would be open to speculation about either intentional or unintentional experimenter (in this case, expert) bias. It is well established that the outcome of most experiments can be ensured through manipulation of key parameters such as exposure time, distance, lighting, and so forth. Second, who should be the participants in the experiment? How should they be matched to be similar to the eyewitnesses in the actual case? Should the participants then be called into court to testify about their participation in the experiment? Third, most courts would probably rule that the probative value of the results of such an experiment would not outweigh their prejudicial effect on the jury (*People v. Brandon*, 1995; *U.S. v. Amaral*, 1973).

For these and other reasons, conducting a formal experiment explicitly for using the obtained data as part of the expert testimony at trial is a bad idea. Nevertheless, a few trial attorneys have suggested that I conduct such experiments on eyewitness evidence pertaining to their clients, and I would assume that some experts have carried out informal experiments to evaluate their hunches about evidence (see Yarmey & Yarmey, 1993). In some European countries, for example, "suitably qualified psychologists may actually have the opportunity to restage crimes with the actual witnesses involved in order to test the veracity of their statements" (Trankell, 1972).

The Expert's Written Report

The form in which an eyewitness expert presents an evaluation of the eyewitness evidence is an important factor to consider prior to the expert beginning the examination of the case materials. Some experts specify that they must be allowed to write a report based on the documents supplied to them by counsel prior to deciding whether to testify in the trial. Some attorneys specify that the expert evaluation must not take the form of a written report, while others welcome a written report. The advantages and risks of a written report are described below. In some cases where the evidence against a client is particularly strong, an attorney may desire a written report simply to certify compliance with the client's option to obtain expert opinion.

The expert's written report can be used by counsel in pre-trial motions to suppress evidence or to dismiss certain counts against a defendant, or to convince the client to accept a plea-bargain. A written report also provides the expert with a forum to "tell the whole truth" concerning the evaluation of the totality of eyewitness evidence in the case. That is, the expert is not constrained in a written report by the substantive questioning from the attorneys and judge in the courtroom. With the narrative format of a written report, the expert is theoretically free to carry out the intended role as a consultant in the matter. As a result, the court and counsels could obtain some potentially useful information from the expert in a written report that adversary questioning would not elicit or may otherwise inhibit.

The written report typically begins with a clear statement of what the expert evaluation of the eyewitness evidence can and cannot offer, similar to the opening portion of this chapter. The report then contains a discussion of factors that the trier of fact should consider when forming an opinion about the eyewitness evidence in the case. A taxonomy of such factors is presented in Chapter 7, and this list can be used as a menu for selecting issues for discussion in the report. One option is to discuss only those factors that would increase doubt about the accuracy of the eyewitness evidence. Another option is to discuss all factors that are relevant to the case at hand, regardless of whether each factor would or would not raise doubt. One problem with the second option is that some readers of the report might attempt to extract a "plus-and-minus" type assessment from the report, whereas it is difficult, if not impossible to specify which factors should be weighted as counterbalancing which others. With either option, relevant laboratory and field research is to be cited from the expansive eyewitness literature in support of the expert opinion, and limitations of the research for evaluating the current case are to be presented where appropriate.

Aside from the advantages of the written-report option for both counsel and the expert, there are several potential pitfalls with this approach that should be considered. Most of these problems ultimately are related to the discovery regulations under which both the defense and prosecution operate in most jurisdictions. It is important to remember that the expert's evaluation as it appears in a written report is discoverable by the opposing counsel and can be quoted in open court. This is particularly problematic with a written report when some information contained in the documents provided initially by counsel is found later to be erroneous or incomplete through further investigation prior to the appearance of the expert. It also is possible that the expert will misinterpret some ambiguous information contained in the documents that is then clarified at trial through the witnesses' testimony. Any of these errors could alter the expert's evaluation of the evidence after the report has been prepared.

Given the somewhat malleable nature of the eyewitness evidence prior to trial and at trial, the counsel who retains an eyewitness expert could be faced with the additional task of explaining an expert evaluation that was based on initially incomplete, ambiguous, or erroneous information. This happened in one case where I had prepared a 12-page, single-spaced report based on one eyewitness account. The eyewitness changed his story on a key point at trial. During cross-examination, the opposing counsel read from my report and shouted "Doctor, why would you submit a report in a case like this when you don't even have the facts straight!" Keep in mind that all that the jurors knew at that point was what the witness had said in front of them at trial. Of course, the retaining counsel corrected the matter on re-direct, but the impression of sloppy work or that the jury knew the eyewitness better than the expert may have been left behind. All of this can be avoided, of course, by the retaining counsel providing the expert with transcripts or relevant summaries of the witnesses' testimony at trial right up to the time of the expert's testimony. I have found in many cases, however, that such updates are not forthcoming unless I specifically request them.

Second, specific statements contained in a written report may be taken out of context by the opposing counsel and used at trial in a manner that does not give the expert an opportunity to offer clarification. Third, the counsel may simply want to avoid discovery of an expert evaluation that is presented in a fashion that is unfavorable to his/her client's case. For any of these reasons, it may be preferable in some, if not most cases to forego a written report in lieu of candid but confidential consultation with counsel and subsequent expert testimony at trial. If the expert is directed by the retaining counsel to not write a report, then the court might compel the expert to prepare a report at some point depending upon the expert's common practice in providing reports in other cases. To date, I have prepared a report at the retaining counsel's request in only two percent of the cases to which I have been appointed. Given the content of eyewitness expert testimony, a written report simply is not necessary in most cases. No evaluation of the eyewitnesses themselves is rendered, and the likely factors and relevant research to be discussed in the testimony are laid out in this handbook as well as in other summaries (see Deffenbacher, 1991 and Penrod et al., 1995).

One final note, an expert should never, ever refer to his/her role as being to "educate the jury" in a written report. This condescending phrase often appears in published articles on eyewitness expert testimony which are intended for other experts, not jurors. Instead, the expert's role is to "discuss with the jury factors that are generally believed to reliably affect a significant percentage of eyewitnesses."

4

Beginning a Case

The courts in some jurisdictions have empowered a committee of judges and administrators to maintain a roster of panel experts who are acceptable to the court on the basis of the committee's established criteria. The establishment of such panels expedites the process of obtaining expert testimony in several ways. On the one hand, the task of counsel to locate a suitable expert is minimized. With respect to the first Amaral criterion (see Chapter 2), the task of the court to determine whether the proposed witness is a recognized expert in the field is reduced to one of ensuring that the witness continues to perform in a professional manner acceptable to the court. Court panels do not formally exclude other potential experts from participating in the system, however, and those persons can be put forth by counsel for consideration by the judge in any case. In fact, the recent Royal Commission Report in the U.K. (Runciman, 1993) rejected the introduction of the "court expert" on the grounds that it might curtail the rigorous examination of the evidence. Even when appointed by the court at the request of one side, the expert often is seen as an "invited intruder" by the court. That is, the court invites the expert, but would rather not have one present.

Rule 702 of the Federal Rules of Evidence specifies that a qualified expert will have "expertise gained by knowledge, skill, experience, training, or education." The threshold appointment criteria used by judges to evaluate a proposed eyewitness expert include the following factors: Professional degrees held, scholarly publications in the field of expertise, relevant instructor positions, relevant awards and certificates of recognition, past history of qualifying in court as an expert, and fee structure. Previous testimony as a recognized expert followed by fee structure appear to be the two criteria most often considered at the outset given current fiscal concerns. However, it is my understanding that judges do compare notes on their observations of specific experts and blatantly adversarial testimony in court is readily recognized by judges. These observations eventually produce a sort of "survival of the fittest" among experts (Loftus, 1986).

As an advocate, counsel makes one decision about whether to obtain an appointment order for a particular expert, makes a second decision about the form in which the expert's opinion will be obtained, and makes a third decision about whether to call the expert to testify at trial. The expert provides input toward each of the three decisions and ultimately decides whether to agree with each of the decisions made by counsel.

The first decision by counsel to obtain an appointment order and the expert's corresponding decision to accept the case typically are made following a brief discussion of the facts of the case initiated by counsel over the telephone. This initial exchange can be a point of friction if counsel is not well organized and succinct with the issues most relevant to the expert's evaluation. Chapter 7 provides counsel with a checklist of sorts, by which potential areas for expert testimony can be organized for presentation in the initial contact with the expert. This exercise also provides an opportunity for counsel to consider the advantages and disadvantages of calling an expert in the case. As discussed in Chapter 2, it is important that counsel confine the use of eyewitness experts to cases where the eyewitness evidence is central to the case, and where the eyewitness evidence is not convincingly supported by other kinds of evidence. In fact, this standard is applicable to passing the "probative value" criterion for admitting the expert testimony (*People v. McDonald,* 1984).

Some experts prefer to be appointed to a case prior to receiving and reviewing any information about the case. This procedure circumvents the problem of "long-winded" attorneys and ensures that the expert will be paid for all of the time spent discussing the case, whether or not the collaboration goes forth any further. The expert, on the other hand, must consider the time constraints that some counsels must work under on some cases when evaluating whether or not to consider an over-the-phone screening of a case. If retained by a private attorney on behalf of a non-indigent client, the expert should obtain a retainer before beginning examination of the documents. When the retainer is expended, the expert should obtain a new one. The expert should never deal directly with the defendant, but rather request that the retainer be provided by the attorney's office through the attorney's holding of funds. This request may seem uncomfortable and the attorney may be famous and charming, but this practice is good fiscal procedure and it prevents the expert from worrying about whether or not he/she will be paid while on the witness stand. One scenario on point is where the defendant post-dated the retainer check, the check bounced after work was done by the expert, the defense strategy changed away from mistaken identification, and the expert was left without compensation for any of the work completed.

From the counsel's perspective, it is advisable to obtain the services of an expert who has at least as much knowledge of standard police procedures as does the attorney. Even if the potential expert appears on the court's panel roster, it is wise either to obtain a copy of the expert's resume or to inquire over the phone as to knowledge of police procedures. The attorney also should take responsibility to ensure adequate preparation of the expert for cross-examination in this area. It even has been suggested that persons who desire to present eyewitness expert testimony in court should first complete relevant police academy courses concerning identification procedures and interview techniques (Hastie, 1986). At a minimum, an expert should read carefully the manual on how to properly conduct identification procedures designed for law enforcement by Wells (1988).

The second decision concerns the form in which the expert opinion will be obtained, either a written report or a confidential verbal consultation. The advantages and pitfalls of a written report for both counsel and expert are presented in Chapter 3. If your jurisdiction follows a reciprocal discovery rule, as does California, then the expert might be compelled to prepare a report at some point by the court depending upon the expert's common practice in providing reports in other cases. Regarding the third decision as to whether the expert will testify at trial, either the expert or counsel will terminate their collaboration whenever the outcome appears not to be advantageous or acceptable to either party. The counsel will terminate the collaboration primarily for adversarial concerns and the expert will terminate the collaboration primarily for ethical concerns related to the role of consultant. Ultimately, the counsel must ask "What would you say if I asked you..." and the expert is obliged to respond with "the whole truth" rather than to become "part of the defense (prosecution) team." The social and financial pressures for the expert to cross this line are substantial, but neither side will ultimately benefit from these transgressions. Testimony that is blatantly adversarial from an expert in court is usually obvious to a judge or jury, and as such it will discounted at several levels. See Chapters 8, 9, and 10 for suggested strategies for presenting expert testimony at trial.

It has been my experience that many of the cases that are referred to eyewitness experts are of the "nice try" variety, where counsel elects to have an expert take a look at the evidence in the off chance that there is something problematic with the eyewitness evidence in the case. Carrying out this process is to ensure that the defendant's option to retain an eyewitness expert has been pursued. This process has become increasingly more standard given the new "three strikes" legislation. I estimate that one fifth of the cases that I have reviewed on behalf of defendants to date would fall into this category, and as such sometimes have not required testimony from an expert. In one case, for example, a defendant was accused of an armed robbery in a public place and was identified independently from a fair photoarray by 16 victims. In a death penalty case, the defendant was identified independently from a fair photoarray by 4 witnesses and his fingerprints were found on the victim's credit cards.

Attention now turns to brief overviews of the status of eyewitness research (Chapter 5) and eyewitness expert testimony (Chapter 6), followed in turn by a detailed description of procedures for applying the results of the research toward an expert evaluation of eyewitness evidence from police and court documents.

5

Current Status of Eyewitness Research

Thousands of research studies have been carried out within the domain of eyewitness psychology. I estimate that there are currently well over 100 papers published in scholarly, peer-reviewed journals and edited books each year. Whether the empirical knowledge base is sufficiently well developed for presentation in a court of law has been debated at least since the turn of the century, and continues to be the source of some debate today. The current status of the debate is discussed in Chapter 6. The strengths and limitations of a variety of populations of eyewitnesses have been studied under a variety of conditions in a variety of settings.

There are two basic types of research studies that form the empirical basis for eyewitness expert testimony, laboratory experiments and field studies. Laboratory experiments are not necessarily conducted in a laboratory, but rather they are carried out using simulated crimes rather than real crimes. These simulated crimes are sometimes staged in a real-world setting without the "witnesses" being forewarned about the staged nature of the event. Sometimes the ruse of realism is carried forward through the investigative interview and identification process. Field studies are carried out with data obtained from actual crimes with real crime victims and witnesses. For several reasons, laboratory studies far outnumber field studies but the pool of recent field studies is substantial. There are advantages and limitations to either laboratory or field studies alone, and therefore a combination of both is desired to obtain a more clear and accurate assessment of factors that are likely to affect eyewitness performance. This comprehensive investigative approach has been widely advocated among social scientists and is followed by many to ensure "convergent validity" among the studies (Davies, 1992).

Some experimental psychologists refer to archival studies as a third type of research procedure. Archival studies are conducted on data from actual crimes, but the data have been filed as police reports and archived by persons other than the researcher who now aggregates and analyzes the data from the files. Farrington and Lambert (1993) and Tollestrup et al. (1994), for example, used police records to compare the descriptions of perpetrators given by victims and witnesses with the actual appearance of the offenders when they were convicted or confessed. In light of the similarities, archival studies will be discussed here as falling under the rubric of field studies.

Laboratory Studies

In laboratory experiments, the event in question is contrived by the researcher. Sometimes the event is a simulated crime presented on videotape. In that case, the persons who serve as eyewitnesses know that they are not actually experiencing a crime. In other studies, the event is a live, staged scenario. In that case, sometimes the persons who serve as eyewitnesses are aware that the event is only staged, whereas sometimes they are led to believe that the event is real. In all cases, the eyewitnesses are tested in some manner about the event after a time delay. The time delay is sometimes within minutes after the event and sometimes after days or weeks. The test might be to recall as much as the witness can about the event, or to work with a sketch artist, or to form a composite image, or to select someone's photo from an array of photos, or to select someone from a live or videotaped lineup. The eyewitnesses are drawn from a variety of populations including college students, non-college educated adults, retarded persons, and people of different races, occupations, and ages including young children and the elderly.

Different eyewitnesses are presented different versions of the event and/or variations of the testing procedure so that theories about the effects of certain factors of interest can be studied. A taxonomy of these factors, which includes witness characteristics, perpetrator characteristics, event characteristics, and the conditions under which a witness is tested, is presented in Chapter 7. The performance of different eyewitnesses is measured under different testing conditions or following a different version of the event such that the effects of the manipulated factors can be assessed. An attempt is made to manipulate each factor independently of any others in an experiment such that any differences in the performance of the eyewitnesses can be attributed to that factor. When two or more factors are varied together, the researcher cannot determine which factor caused the effect on eyewitness performance, and the experiment is said to be "confounded."

For example, a researcher would not want to manipulate level of stress by manipulating the distance that eyewitnesses are placed from the event. This is because any observed difference in performance between eyewitnesses could be due either to stress or to distance from the event. Instead, the researcher would want to develop different versions of the same event that would result in different levels of stress reported by the eyewitnesses while keeping all other factors equivalent such as distance for view. Any observed differences in performance by witnesses who view the different versions of the event could then be more likely ascribed to stress and not something else. However, a researcher can never be completely sure that differences in performance seen in any one experiment were caused by the intended manipulation. Therefore, it is important to compare the outcomes of several studies that were designed to assess the effects of one factor such as stress under a variety of conditions. This approach is called meta-analysis of experiments. With the data base that is currently available in eyewitness psychology, meta-analyses are possible for several of the factors presented in Chapter 7. A meta-analysis is a study of data from several different experiments using one overall analysis, where each experiment was designed to study the same factor.

A major advantage of laboratory studies is that the researcher has control over what happened in the event. With this control, the researcher is able to accurately assess whether the witness's performance is accurate or not. A second advantage is that the different factors that make up a crime event can be studied separately, again because the researcher has control over what happened at each staging of the event. A third advantage is that many witnesses can be studied to the same event, not just one or two who happen to proceed through the system and thus appear in police and court records.

The major limitation of laboratory studies is that the element of realism is only approximated in the entire process. Although some laboratory studies have been carried out where the witnesses were led to believe that they were participants in an actual crime event and investigation (Hosch, Leippe, Marchioni, & Cooper, 1984; Hosch & Platz, 1984), there are strict ethical regulations against creating the level of psychological trauma to research participants that one would expect with some real crimes (American Psychological Association, 1981).

Field Studies

With few exceptions, the limitations of laboratory studies become the advantages of the field studies and the advantages of laboratory studies become the limitations of the field studies. By definition, the element of realism is present in field studies because both the event and the testing procedures are real, and not staged or simulated. However, the researcher does not have any control over what happened in the event with an actual crime. Therefore, with the exception of some crimes that are videotaped via security systems, accurate scoring of the eyewitness performance in field experiments is limited to certain forms of corroboration that may be imperfect, such as confessions, physical evidence, and reports from many other witnesses. Analyses of archival data also are dependent on these limited forms of corroboration. Furthermore, there is the potential for a case selection artifact in these analyses because many of the available cases were never solved and there is no way of establishing the accuracy of the events as described or the appearance of the suspects. Perhaps, for example, eyewitnesses are more likely to be accurate in cases where there was enough evidence to successfully apprehend and prosecute the perpetrators. If so, then an analysis of those cases alone would produce witness accuracy rates that are higher than what is true in reality.

The researcher also has no control over which factors are present in a real event in combination with which others. With this lack of control, it sometimes is difficult to determine which factor has affected eyewitness performance in an actual crime. As an example, one often cited field study showed that the eyewitnesses who were most stressed were the most accurate in their recollections of a real-world crime event (Yuille & Cutshall, 1986). This finding is significant because many laboratory studies and some other field studies show the opposite result, that extreme stress hinders performance (see Chapter 7). In this one study, however, the witnesses who were most stressed also were the ones who were the closest in proximity to the event. Thus, it cannot be concluded whether those persons who expressed the most stress were more accurate because they were under a heightened state of arousal or because they were closer to the event and thus had a better opportunity to observe. In another field study of actual cases, it was found that the probability of an eyewitness making a selection from a photoarray dropped by 40 percent when a deadly weapon was used in the crime (Tollestrup et al., 1994). While this finding lends support for the phenomenon of weapon focus, other factors could have caused this effect that accompanied the presence or absence of a weapon in the crimes.

There has been much debate over the somewhat unavoidable tradeoff between realism in field studies and experimental control in laboratory studies specifically in the domain of eyewitness psychology (Bekerian, 1993; Murray & Wells, 1982). The argument that laboratory studies do not tell us much about the real world is often raised by opposing counsels on cross-examination (see Chapter 9). To my knowledge, the opposite argument, that field studies do not tell us much about which specific factors reliably affect eyewitness performance, has not been raised by counsels on any regular basis in court. Such an argument, while having some merit, probably would be more difficult to explain to a jury.

6

Current Status of Eyewitness Expert Testimony

Psychologists and other social scientists who have been involved in the study of eyewitness performance do not all agree that eyewitness experts serve a valuable function in legal proceedings at the present time. One psychologist concluded that "it is misrepresentation...not to tell juries that the effects about which one is testifying have little or no empirical basis, or great variability, or little or no evidence of generalization" (Elliott, 1993, p. 434). Nevertheless, surveys of social scientists who would likely qualify as eyewitness experts show a general agreement that enough is known about the kinds of factors discussed in Chapter 7 to allow for expert testimony to be offered in court (Kassin et al., 1989; Yarmey & Jones, 1983). Some of the arguments that have been raised in the debate are presented below, but for additional discussion, see the following three sources: *The American Psychologist*, May issue, 1983; *Law and Human Behavior*, June issue, 1986; and *The American Psychologist*, May issue, 1993.

The Issues

(1) Ecological Validity of Eyewitness Research: "Many research studies bear little resemblance to the real world. Many of the studies on eyewitness performance are conducted with

events that are not like real crimes; and furthermore, college students who often know that the event is not a real crime typically serve as the witnesses in exchange for course credit (Yuille, 1993). What, then, do these studies tell us about eyewitnesses in real crime situations?"

This criticism of eyewitness psychology stems from a more general call by a number of modern cognitive psychologists for research studies that are more generalizable to real world settings. Here is how Eysenck (1984) put it: "Of 59 basic cognitive phenomena, only two have immediate relevance, one relates to chess playing, and the other to looking at the moon. ...[T]he more successful we are in examining part of the cognitive system in isolation, the less our data are likely to tell us about cognition in everyday life" (pp. 363-364).

Eysenck's (1984) observation underscores the importance of conducting field studies on eyewitness performance as well as laboratory experiments that preserve many of the elements which are present in real crimes and real crime investigations. Laboratory experiments typically are designed to isolate a particular factor for study under highly controlled conditions so that its effect, if any, can be assessed independently of the variety of other factors that appear in the real world. Laboratory experiments are necessary to establish the existence of phenomena that may be counterintuitive and, as such, are least well understood by the layman. Once an effect of a factor is observed, then it is important to replicate the effect under more realistic conditions.

Fortunately, more ecologically valid laboratory studies have been conducted in eyewitness psychology in recent years and the available field studies have the potential to validate the laboratory observations. Further, not all laboratory studies have been conducted with college students. While college students have been the "fruit flies" for much research in psychology in general, I have studied children, non-college adult samples, and mentally retarded persons as eyewitnesses. Other researchers have studied additional populations such as the elderly (Bartlett & Leslie, 1986; Mello & Fisher, 1995; Scogin, Calhoon, & E'Errico, 1994; Yarmey & Kent, 1980). Moreover, some experiments have been carried out with a broad spectrum of individuals specifically to assess "who remembers best" (Loftus, Levidow, & Duensing, 1992). The myth still exists, however, among some counsels that social scientists only study college students, or even worse. In 1993, for example, I was asked on cross-examination, "Isn't it true Dr. Geiselman that most of your studies have been conducted with rats?"

Aside from the fact that considerable attention has been given to a variety of populations in eyewitness psychology, no significant differences in eyewitness performance have been found between college and non-college adult samples of witnesses (Geiselman, Fisher, MacKinnon, & Holland, 1986). Students have been found to perform no differently from other groups on a variety of eyewitness tasks (Loftus et al., 1992).

In addition, not all laboratory studies are far removed from real world conditions. High rates of false identifications have been observed in staged-crime experiments where the ruse of being genuine criminal investigations was maintained and where the observers were not forewarned that they would be witnesses (Clifford & Scott, 1978; Foster, Libkulman, Schooler, & Loftus, 1994; Hosch et al., 1984; Krafka & Penrod, 1985; Malpass & Devine, 1980; Murray & Wells, 1982). In some cases, the observers believed at the time of their identification decisions that the crime was authentic (a bicycle theft, a theft of their own watches, an attack with a letter-opener) and that there would be consequences to the accused.

There is some need for caution in extrapolating findings from laboratory studies to real world settings, however. Some psychologists have argued that laboratory experiments underestimate the capacity of actual eyewitnesses of crime (Yuille, 1993). Consider the following laboratory experiment. Buckhout (1974) showed a videotape of a staged purse snatching on WNBC Television in New York. Following a break, viewers were shown a lineup of six persons and were encouraged to phone in to identify the perpetrator from the lineup or to state that he was not in the lineup. Two-thousand one-hundred forty-five viewers phoned in, but only 14 percent correctly selected the perpetrator who was in position two. This percentage is no greater than would be expected on the basis of the viewers having guessed. The results of this experiment paint a rather dismal picture of eyewitness performance; nearly 2,000 witnesses were wrong!

In contrast, my own field study of actual crimes in Miami, Florida, showed that 85 percent of the statements made by the witnesses were accurate, at least for the limited elements of the crimes that could be corroborated or disproved by other evidence. On the basis of these results, I wrote that "if this difference between laboratory and field studies continues to appear, one may question the validity of describing in court the accuracy rates found in the laboratory as evidence of general unreliability of eyewitness testimony in the field" (Fisher, Geiselman, & Amador, 1989). This is not to imply, however, that real-world conditions always have favored superior eyewitness performance. Other crimes of violence have not yielded such high levels of overall accuracy and the errors and confusions typically observed in laboratory experiments have occurred (Davies, 1992). Furthermore, rates of misidentification appear to be much lower in laboratory studies than in more realistic crime enactments (Lindsay & Harvie, 1988), while correct recognition of persons appears to be appreciably higher in laboratory settings (Shapiro & Penrod, 1986).

(2) Reliability of Eyewitness Research: "The results from studies of any given eyewitness factor are not consistent from experiment to experiment. How then, are experimental psychologists to testify in court about the effect of that factor on eyewitness performance?"

In response to this question, Kassin, Ellsworth, & Smith (1994) stated that "any scientific phenomenon can be debunked by citing a null result or an isolated failure to replicate, or by narrowing the range of studies that qualify for inclusion. So what?" In agreement, the U.S. Supreme Court noted in *Daubert* that scientific knowledge need not be "known to a certainty" (p. 2796) to qualify as foundation for expert opinion. From *Daubert*, Melton (1995) concluded that while the debate about the reliability or validity of psychological evidence may comment on the state of the field, "it is largely irrelevant to the question of admissibility of psychologists' opinions." It is true that not all studies in the vast literature of eyewitness psychology on any given factor have produced the same results. For example, there are some studies showing a negative effect of stress, some showing a positive effect of stress, and some showing no significant effect of stress on eyewitness performance (Deffenbacher, 1983). Differences in the nature of the event and the methodology by which the experiment is carried out, as well as simple chance, have led to different outcomes. If the distribution of outcomes presents a balanced distribution of outcomes, then no reliable conclusion can be drawn from the set of available studies. However, if the distribution of outcomes is significantly skewed in either the positive or negative direction, then a conclusion can be drawn from the group of studies.

Consider the set of available studies that has addressed the "weapon focus" effect in eyewitness psychology. Weapon focus refers to the tendency for some eyewitnesses to focus their attention on a weapon at the exclusion of other details that were present at the time of the event. McCloskey and Egeth (1993) point out that of the available studies, only one-third of them show a negative weapon-focus like effect on eyewitness performance (citing a meta-analysis by Steblay, 1992). The other two-thirds of the studies show no significant effect on performance. In sum, the presence of a weapon often had no effect on performance, but when it did, the effect was to hinder eyewitness performance and decrease the frequency of accurate identifications. Contrary to the myth that "I'll never forget his face because he pointed a gun right at me," none of the studies showed the presence of a weapon to enhance performance. Thus, eyewitness expert testimony has probative value in this instance because the distribution of outcomes runs counter to a common misconception about the effect of the presence of a weapon on eyewitness performance (Kassin & Barndollar, 1992; Lindsay, 1994; Loftus, 1979). This is the case even though the studies are not unanimous in their outcome.

There are exceptions to each of the factors included in the taxonomy of influences on eyewitness performance presented in Chapter 7. Some of the exceptions are cited there and objective eyewitness expert testimony will include an acknowledgment that these exceptions exist.

(3) The Probabilistic Nature of Eyewitness Research: "The eyewitness expert can tell the jury little, if anything about the reliability of the particular eyewitnesses in any given case. Of what practical use, then, is the expert testimony to the trier of fact?"

The specificity element of this assertion is almost universally true. Law is concerned primarily with the outcome of a given case, whereas empirical psychology is concerned with deriving general principles that encompass a variety of individual instances but do not necessarily predict the outcome of a single case. It is argued at several points in this book that the eyewitness expert probably would gain little from an in-person examination of the eyewitnesses, and the expert should not offer testimony as to the accuracy of any particular eyewitness in court. *The Specialty Guidelines for Forensic Psychologists* (American Psychological Association, 1991) further precludes testimony about the psychological characteristics of particular individuals without an opportunity to conduct an examination of the individual adequate to the scope of the opinions.

The probabilistic nature of eyewitness research has led some legal scholars to argue that it has little to contribute to the jury's decision-making task (King, 1986) and this problem has been listed as one of the principal dilemmas in the field of psychology and law (Wrightsman, Nietzel, & Fortune, 1994). It is a difficult task indeed to explain to a jury the probabilistic nature of research findings in the context of what these findings can offer them in deciding the case at hand. As one social scientist has cautioned, eyewitness experts should avoid telling the jury about "the average witness" because someone just might ask the expert to point to an average witness in the courtroom (Bekerian, 1993). Instead, the eyewitness expert must present factors that are relevant to the case which are generally believed to reliably affect a significant percentage of eyewitnesses. Common cross-examination of experts on this issue is discussed in Chapter 8.

(4) Eyewitness Psychology as Common Knowledge: "Much of what the eyewitness expert is prepared to tell a jury is not beyond the common experience of the jurors. Everyone has had experience with remembering events and as a result of this experience, most jurors recognize the limitations of memory. What, then, can the expert tell jurors that they do not already know?"

As discussed in Chapter 2, some courts have considered this issue as it relates to the "proper subject matter" criterion from the Amaral decision, and some courts have agreed with the premise that eyewitness expert testimony is not beyond the common experience of the jury (*U.S. v. Rincon*, 1993). What can be cited in response are the results of survey studies which indicate that laypersons eligible for jury duty often do not agree with recognized experts as to the typical effects of key situational factors on eyewitness performance (Brigham & Bothwell, 1983; Deffenbacher & Loftus, 1982; Kassin & Barndollar, 1992; Lindsay, 1994; Loftus, 1979; Ramirez et al., 1995; Saks & Hastie, 1978; Wells, 1984; Yarmey & Jones, 1983). For example, a significantly greater percentage of laypersons than experts believe that eyewitness confidence should strongly predict accuracy, that law-enforcement professionals make better witnesses, and that cross-racial identification is not a significant problem. These findings have been confirmed in surveys, studies where laypersons are asked to predict the outcome of experiments, and in mock-jury studies where the quality of the eyewitnessing and identification conditions are manipulated.

The validity of the data from surveys of laypersons has been challenged (Konecni & Ebbesen, 1986; Wells, 1984). The validity of data from any survey study is contingent in part on the way in which the questions are posed to the respondents. If the question-answer alternatives are biased, so will be the results. In the case of eyewitness performance, however, significant differences between experts and laypersons have been observed in their responses to the same questions, such as questions about cross-race identification (Yarmey & Jones, 1983). With this being the case, it would have to be argued further that the laypersons somehow interpreted the alternative responses to the questions differently than the experts. I have not detected jargon-laden wording in either the questions or the alternative answers used in the available surveys.

Furthermore, the survey data from laypersons is not the only indicator that eyewitness psychology is not common knowledge. Corroborating results have been obtained in controlled, mock-trial experiments with persons eligible for jury duty serving as mock jurors (Lindsay, 1994). Mock jurors have been found to be insensitive even to the effects of biased lineup instructions in producing false eyewitness identifications (Wells, 1984). Mock jurors also have been found to believe that identifications based on voice are just as likely to be accurate as identifications based on viewing a lineup, whereas the available data show identifications from voice alone to be significantly less accurate (McAllister, Hunter, Dale, & Keay, 1993). Jurors consistently overestimate the accuracy of eyewitness identifications, especially when the witnesses are confident, and they undervalue viewing conditions that experts believed to predict eyewitness accuracy. Nevertheless, I agree with what I interpret to be the perception of some experts that juror ignorance is somewhat overrated (Bermant, 1986). In fact, the available surveys have found that laypersons sometimes agree with the experts on the effects of some eyewitness factors. Kassin and Barndollar (1992), for example, found that a somewhat greater percentage of laypersons than experts agreed that extreme stress can interfere with eyewitness performance, and just as many laypersons as experts agreed with a statement about weapon focus. Concern still remains as to whether jurors will make systematic use of the knowledge they do possess in arriving at their decisions (Lindsay, 1994).

(5) Lack of General Explanatory Theories: "Some of the phenomena that are routinely described in eyewitness expert testimony are not accompanied by any explanatory theory that has general acceptance among the community of eyewitness researchers. Therefore, the expert testimony does not pass one of the four criteria established in *U.S. v. Amaral* (1973)."

As discussed in Chapter 2, the notion of a generally accepted explanatory theory is an elusive one for the entire field of psychology. Certain eyewitness phenomena appear to be reliable yet there is no consensus among researchers as to why these phenomena occur. For example, there is considerable laboratory evidence that same-race identifications tend to be more accurate than cross-race identifications (Bothwell, Brigham, & Malpass, 1989; Malpass & Kravitz, 1969; Shapiro & Penrod, 1986; Shepherd & Deregowski, 1981), yet the source of the cross-race effect continues to be debated. The effect does not seem to be a function of frequency of contact with the other race (Malpass & Kravitz, 1969; Ng & Lindsay, 1994), but children who live in mixed-race environments tend to show less of a cross-race effect (Ferman & Entwistle, 1976). Adults who have very close friends of the other race also show less of a cross-race effect, suggesting that the quality of the exposure may make a difference (Lavrakas, Buri, & Mayzner, 1976; Lindsay & Wells, 1983). Numerous explanatory theories have been put forth, but no single theory has emerged as a generally accepted explanation.

There does not appear to be any simple solution to this dilemma as it relates to eyewitness psychologists testifying in court about cross-racial identification. A significant majority of experts in the field agree that the phenomenon is sufficiently reliable to be presented in court (Kassin et al., 1989; Kassin & Barndollar, 1992; Yarmey & Jones, 1983), but opponents of eyewitness expert testimony continue to make the point that there is no generally accepted explanatory theory about cross-racial identification (McCloskey & Egeth, 1993). Thus, the "explanatory theory" issue as it relates to some eyewitness factors is especially open to interpretation by the courts.

Based on past applications of the related Frye standard (*U.S. v. Frye*, 1923), however, it would be expected that most courts will continue to focus on the implied reliability concern rather than the explanatory theory requirement. If this is the case, then expert testimony about such factors as cross-racial identification will continue to be admitted. In fact, the recent *Daubert* decision (1993) has shifted the attention of judges away from the general repute of theories and toward the reliability of the research. Reliability can be evaluated on the basis of scientifically respected control studies, peer reviews, and falsifiability of the results. Falsifiability refers to whether or not an experiment can be designed to show that a theory is not true. The Supreme Court expressed confidence in effective cross-examination as a means for attacking shaky but admissible expert evidence. Hence, counsels and judges must become more conversant on research methodology and procedures in eyewitness psychology.

(6) Disturbing the Balance for Convictions: "Eyewitness expert testimony may be prejudicial to the outcome of legal proceedings in that it has the potential to increase the number of guilty parties who are freed from conviction."

The validity of this premise is dependent on how it is framed in the context of several factors including the frequency with which the prosecution calls an eyewitness expert relative to the defense, the quality of the expert testimony (as opposed to its adversarial success), and the critic's beliefs about the ability of juries to utilize expert testimony to evaluate the eyewitness evidence. Experts also disagree as to the probable frequency with which innocent persons are wrongfully convicted, with some sources claiming sizable numbers (Huff et al., 1986; Loftus & Ketcham, 1991) while others claim that these occurrences are extremely rare (Konecni & Ebbesen, 1986; Moore, 1993). Konecni and Ebbesen (1986) estimate that there are probably no more than one wrongful conviction based on faulty eyewitness testimony in California every three years. Of course, there is no way of knowing how many there really are.

It is the case that eyewitness experts are rarely called to testify on behalf of the prosecution (Kassin et al., 1989). I rarely have been asked to testify for the prosecution, but I have been asked on several occasions to aid in the preparation of cases for the prosecution out of court. I assume that other social scientists have been asked to provide similar services. While it is possible that some persons who have qualified as eyewitness experts have offered blatantly adversarial testimony for the defense that is inaccurate or misleading, such experts, as well as experts who could be similarly classified for the prosecution, are not likely to survive the sustained scrutiny that is available at several levels in the legal system (Loftus, 1986).

Finally, the results of some mock-trial studies have shown that eyewitness expert testimony can cause skepticism on the part of many jurors about the reliability of eyewitness testimony (Cutler, Dexter, & Penrod, 1990; Lindsay, 1994; Wells, Lindsay, & Tousignant, 1980). However, there also are studies that show increased juror sensitivity to eyewitness viewing and identification conditions as a result of testimony from an eyewitness expert (Cutler, Penrod, & Dexter, 1989; Wells & Wright, 1983). In addition, there are no viable alternatives to eyewitness expert testimony at present. Judge's cautionary instructions to the jury have yet to be modeled in a form that improves juror sensitivity to eyewitnessing conditions (see Chapter 13). In the absence of a viable alternative, expert testimony that serves to undermine the testimony of credible eyewitnesses can be neutralized through effective cross-examination or through testimony by rival experts putting forth the other view.

The "Battle of the Experts"

Given the debate among scholars within the field of eyewitness psychology, one possible outcome of the routine introduction of eyewitness expert testimony is the creation of adversarial experts who then engage in a "battle of the experts" in court. Given this possibility, a major concern of the court is the unnecessary expenditure of public funds to obtain eyewitness expert testimony that contradicts other eyewitness expert testimony (*U.S. v. Amaral*, 1973). The effect of a battle of the experts could be a neutralization of the testimony (Doyle, 1984). A complementary concern of some psychologists is the "bad image" that these battles might give to the entire discipline of psychology (McCloskey & Egeth, 1983) and that they will weaken the perceived value of the testimony in the eyes of the court (Bazelon, 1982). While these concerns perhaps have some merit, they apply to other areas of expert testimony including the testimony of mental health professionals (Loftus, 1986). Furthermore, research on the practices of psychological experts by Champagne, Shuman, and Whitaker (1992) failed to reveal an industry of "hired guns" who obtain most of their income through expert referral sources and advertisements leading to their compensated testimony in court.

In any case, Loftus (1986) has encouraged the battle to take place and believes that it would be good for the process in the long run. She writes: "We should not put off adversarial confrontation. We should encourage the 'other side' to appear, urge them to present their best evidence, and force the triers of fact to look hard at the data." A few battles between experts have already taken place, such as in *People v. Pacely* (1984) between Dr. Loftus and Dr. Ebbesen, where the testimony on behalf of the prosecution focused mainly on conflicting experimental outcomes. In *U.S. v. Downing* (1985), opposing experts debated whether the existing literature on human learning and memory is relevant to crime situations. Penrod et al. (1995) envision that such arguments about the scientific basis of eyewitness expert testimony are likely to be more common in the wake of the *Daubert* ruling (1993).

Given the current reluctance of the prosecution to call eyewitness experts to testify at trial, however, an overt battle of the experts may be confined mainly to academia. Behind the scenes battles will continue to take the form of some experts consulting with the prosecution to prepare prosecutors for their cross-examination of other experts who would testify for the defense. Given the likelihood of this chain of events, Chapter 9 is devoted to cross-examination questioning of eyewitness experts and Chapter 10 is devoted to re-direct questioning in response to cross. First, however, a discussion is presented of a taxonomy of factors that are thought to reliably affect eyewitness performance.

7

Evaluation of Eyewitness Factors

The Three Stages of Human Information Processing

Factors that are generally believed to reliably affect the performance of a significant percentage of eyewitnesses can be conveniently organized in terms of three stages of information processing. These stages are commonly used by some eyewitness experts at the beginning of direct examination questioning to provide a structure for a subsequent discussion of the eyewitness factors that are relevant to the case at hand (see Chapter 8). The first stage, labeled acquisition or encoding, concerns factors that are present at the time of the event. These include characteristics of the eyewitnesses, victims, and perpetrators, as well as key elements of the crime event itself. For example, eyewitnesses who are intoxicated at the time of the crime appear to be less accurate in their recollections about persons than sober witnesses (Read et al., 1992; Yuille & Tollestrup, 1990) and eyewitnesses classified as being neurotic have shown a similar deficit (Zanni & Offermann, 1978).

The second stage, labeled retention, concerns factors that might influence the nature of eyewitness memory between the time of the event and the time at which the witness must recall the event. These include forgetting with the passage of time, as well as influences from external sources, such as other persons and the press, and internal sources such as the witness's personal reflections and rationalization of the event. The third stage, labeled retrieval, concerns factors that are present when the witness must recall the event. These include the composition of a lineup or photoarray as well as the conditions under which an identification is attempted or a verbal report is given. Verbal descriptions given by eyewitnesses usually are general rather than specific (gender, race, height, weight, hair, age) and tend to include ranges ("early to mid 30s") (Lindsay, Martin, & Webber, 1994; Pigott & Brigham, 1985; Sporer, 1992; Wells, 1985).

Eyewitness memory performance has been found to be influenced by factors that are present at each of the three stages of information processing (Deffenbacher, 1991; Loftus, 1979; Yarmey, 1979). Most of these factors have been found to apply to earwitnessing as well (Deffenbacher, Cross, Handkins, Chance, & others, 1989; Yarmey, 1994; Yarmey, Yarmey, & Yarmey, 1994), except when the voices are uniquely distinct (Wallendael, Surace, Parsons, & Brown, 1994). This is in sharp contrast to what would be expected if memory operated like a videotape recording that could be created, stored, and played back faithfully. In fact, contrary to the common belief, there is no scientific evidence for the videotape analogy (Loftus & Loftus, 1980). Instead, human memories are temporary constructions or interpretations of sensory input from the environment, and these abstractions continue to evolve through thought, rationalization, and further input from others (Gary, Loftus, & Brown, 1994). Memory retrieval is not purely reproductive, but it is reconstructive and sometimes even constructive. That is, elements of some memories are elaborations created by witnesses over time based on their own rationalizations for what must have happened and suggestions from others. Witnesses can become quite confident in these pseudo memories with no awareness of their source. In one case where I served as an expert, a nervous and fearful eyewitness had a "revelation" of a fuzzy memory after 12 interviews containing suggestive interrogation, much speculation in the local media, and some consumption of alcohol.

Some of the factors that influence eyewitness memory are easily understood such as the opportunity that the witness had to view a perpetrator (Reynolds & Pezdek, 1992; Shapiro & Penrod, 1986) and the passage of time before an identification is attempted (Deffenbacher, 1986; Egan, Pittner, & Goldstein, 1977; Tollestrup et al., 1994), while other factors apparently are more obscure to the layman (Brigham & Bothwell, 1983; Lindsay, 1994; Loftus, 1979; Saks & Hastie, 1978; Wells, 1984; Yarmey & Jones, 1983). The effects of some factors, such as stress, cannot be classified as affecting just one particular stage, and may affect memory at all three stages for some witnesses (Deffenbacher, 1991). Expert testimony can be helpful to the trier of fact in matching the conditions of the specific case before the court to the corresponding literature from eyewitness psychology.

A taxonomy of factors commonly included in eyewitness expert testimony is presented below. No attempt is made in this chapter to evaluate that reliability or validity of the studies cited. A discussion of those issues is presented in Chapter 6.

Strategies for cross-examination of the eyewitnesses themselves on some of these factors can be found in Bailey and Rothblatt (1985) and Bailey and Fishman (1995).

Taxonomy of Eyewitness Factors

(1) Stress: The laboratory and field data concerning the effects of stress on cognitive performance are somewhat mixed, with many laboratory studies showing stress to narrow attention (Easterbrook, 1959; Eysenck, 1977; Kahneman, 1973; Loftus & Mackworth, 1978; Maass & Koehnken, 1989). Persons who experience highly emotional events tend to report that images are more vivid, they rehearse the event more frequently, and their confidence in their memories increases (Bekerian & Dennett, 1993). Both laboratory and field studies have shown a negative effect of heightened arousal on face recognition accuracy (Brigham, Maass, Martinez, & Whittenberger, 1983; Clifford & Scott, 1978; Clifford & Hollin, 1981; Hosch & Bothwell, 1990; Peters, 1988).

Clifford and Scott (1978) led participants in a laboratory study to believe that a fight was occurring in the next room. When the fighting stopped, a man came out with either a letter opener and blood on his hands or a pen with ink on his hands. Significantly fewer observers were able to identify the man with the letter opener and blood. Kramer, Buckhout, Fox, Widman, et al. (1991) exposed participants to a traumatic autopsy color slide embedded in a series of travel scenes. The participants were significantly less likely to recall the slides immediately following the autopsy slide than participants who were shown a neutral travel slide in its place. Actual crime victims also tend to overestimate the duration of a crime event (Schneider, Griffith, Sumi, & Burcart, 1978; Yarmey, 1993) and these overestimates are greater with a more stressful event (Loftus, Schooler, Boone, & Kline, 1987).

A significant percentage of eligible jurors believe that victims would be more accurate witnesses than observers due to the added arousal of being a victim (Deffenbacher & Loftus, 1982; Saks & Hastie, 1978), but the opposite has been found in at least one simulation study. With a simulated theft, bystanders later reported more correct information about the perpetrator than did the person who witnessed his own possession being stolen (Kassin, 1984). The researcher reasoned that the emotion generated by being a crime victim interfered with the victim's attention to the details of the crime. In another experiment, where the element of realism was preserved, personalized watch thefts with victim status resulted in no more accurate identifications than impersonal calculator thefts with bystander status (Hosch & Cooper, 1982).

In many cases, the eyewitness is not forewarned of an impending criminal event and might therefore be expected to be immune to the effects of stress. However, there is some evidence that a stressful event can produce negative effects on memory for what was experienced just prior to the event. In a laboratory study by Loftus and Burns (1982), observers watched a bank training video of a bank robbery that ended in the parking lot. In one version, a young boy was shot in the face and slumped to the ground holding his face. In a control condition with other observers, the upsetting ending was replaced by an equally unexpected but innocuous ending. The participants ratings of upset confirmed a significant difference between the two versions of the incident. Visual information presented in both versions just before the ending was significantly less likely to be remembered in the upsetting version. The interference from the upsetting ending was observed for information contained in the video as much as two minutes prior to the ending. The authors concluded that witnessing a traumatic event can interfere with the consolidation of memory for what happened just prior to the event. This phenomenon is commonly referred to as "retroactive interference."

It is important to note that high levels of arousal appear to affect memory for peripheral details more than central details such as the identification of the key figure in a crime (Christianson & Loftus, 1987; Read, Yuille, & Tollestrup, 1992, Exp. 2). Also, one field study has shown a positive correlation between self-reported stress and accurate memory performance (Yuille & Cutshall, 1986). This particular result is difficult to interpret, however, because the witnesses who were the most accurate were the ones who were closest to the perpetrator. Thus, stress was confounded with distance for view, which logically would also affect the accuracy of performance. A second field study of bank robberies in Sweden found no effect of self-reported emotional arousal on memory for certain details such as clothing and weapon, but the victims were more accurate in their identifications than bystanders (Christianson & Hubinette, 1993). Thus, while perhaps the majority of studies show a negative effect of high stress on cognitive performance, there are studies that have failed to show the effect. Whether victims or bystanders are more accurate depends on their relative goodness of view which is a function of several situational factors such as distance, lighting, evoked stress, and focus of attention. Regardless, the pattern of data does not support the belief that victim status reliably enhances eyewitness accuracy.

In addition, one laboratory study using a simulated theft has shown that the negative effects of intoxication on later person identification performance can be counteracted by increasing the level of arousal experienced by the eyewitness during the crime (Read et al., 1992). The authors speculated that the increased arousal served to "sober up" the eyewitnesses.

To explain the differences between studies, some researchers have cited the "Yerkes-Dodson Law," which specifies that an observer's performance decreases with high levels of stress but performance increases with a little stress as compared to sleep-level arousal (Deffenbacher, 1983). In most crime scenarios that appear in a trial, the level of stress would be expected to be on the high or extreme end of the scale thereby producing a negative effect. Other researchers have concluded that the effect of stress on performance depends on a complex interaction between the type of detail (central or peripheral), time of test (with stress, sometimes delayed recall is better), and the retrieval conditions (presence of sufficient retrieval cues, repeated recall attempts) (see Anderson, 1990, Christianson, 1992, and Deffenbacher, 1994, for reviews). There is some evidence that eyewitnesses who could be classified as neurotic are especially affected negatively by high levels of stress (Bothwell, Brigham, & Pigott, 1987). Thus, some individual differences in reaction to stress are to be expected. Other researchers have found in a simulation study with police recruits that while stress decreased the amount of information recalled, the accuracy of what was recalled was not negatively affected (Yuille, Davies, Gibling, & Marxsen, 1994).

Nevertheless, 71 percent of the experts polled in 1989 agreed that the negative effects of stress are sufficiently well established to warrant eyewitness expert testimony in court (Kassin et al., 1989). The results of another survey study suggest that the majority of eligible jurors already believe in the negative effects of extreme stress on witness performance (Kassin & Barndollar, 1992), but laypersons are still more likely to believe that a violent event will be better remembered than a non-violent event (Yarmey & Jones, 1983). It appears that many laypersons confuse a victim's lasting memory that the crime happened to them with the potential accuracy of the victim's identification of the perpetrator.

Related to the issue of stress is the concept of "flashbulb" memories (Brown & Kulik, 1977). This label has been given to memories that arise from significant life events and which persist over an unusually long period of time in comparison to ordinary events (Christianson, 1992). Some have speculated that memory for traumatic episodes, such as a crime event, might be unusually good because of the "flashbulb" effect. However, flashbulb memories, while persistent, are fraught with errors through forgetting, rehearsal, and repeated telling of the event (Loftus & Kaufman, 1992) just as memories for more mundane events. Flashbulb memories appear to be similar to any other memory in that stress affects memory for peripheral details more than central details, and there is a similar breakdown of the relation between witness confidence and accuracy (see factor 3) with flashbulb memories (Neisser & Harsch, 1992).

(2) Weapon Focus: The eyewitness phenomenon of weapon focus is relevant to the evaluation of the testimony of witnesses and victims who were confronted by an armed assailant. Laboratory evidence suggests that under stress, attention tends to narrow (Loftus & Mackworth, 1978), sometimes on a weapon (Johnson & Scott, 1976; Kramer, Buckhout, & Eugenio, 1990; Loftus, Loftus, & Messo, 1987; Maass &

Koehnken, 1987; Skolnick & Shaw, 1994) and sometimes on other central details of an event (Christianson & Loftus, 1987, 1991; Read et al., 1992). Weapon focus has been shown for both victims and bystanders (Loftus, Loftus, & Messo, 1987; Maass & Koehnken, 1987). With such focus, the opportunity for a witness to view and process in memory the face of the perpetrator would theoretically be reduced (Cutler & Penrod, 1988; O'Rourke, Penrod, Cutler, & Stuve, 1989; Tooley, Brigham, Maass, & Bothwell, 1987). The phenomenon of weapon focus has been confirmed in studies of both eyewitnesses' self reports (Tooley et al., 1987) and their eye movements (Loftus et al., 1987). In the Clifford and Scott (1974) laboratory study described in the section above on stress, participants were significantly less likely to identify the male actor from a lineup when they could describe the more dangerous "weapon."

Weapon focus appears to account for a 20-to-30 percent difference in identification accuracy in controlled laboratory studies using videotapes and slide sequences of crimes (Cutler, Penrod, & Martins, 1987; Loftus et al., 1987). In one field study, significantly more police suspects were identified when no weapon was present (73%) than when a weapon was present (30%), showing a 40 percent difference in the likelihood of an actual crime victim/witness selecting the police suspect (Tollestrup et al., 1994). Unfortunately, the accuracy of the identifications typically cannot be corroborated one way or the other in a field study (see Chapter 5), so the effects of weapon focus on identification accuracy cannot be precisely determined. This underscores the importance of the laboratory simulations.

In a meta-analysis of 19 experiments on weapon focus, Steblay (1992) found 6 studies to show a significant effect and 13 to show no effect. Thus, presence of a weapon either had no effect or it adversely affected identification performance. Contrary to myth, in none of the studies did the presence of a weapon enhance performance. Two available surveys suggest that laypersons are less knowledgeable about weapon focus effects than eyewitness experts (Loftus, 1979; Yarmey & Jones, 1983), while one survey showed no difference in sensitivity to this problem (Kassin & Barndollar, 1992).

In theory, the weapon focus phenomenon also would apply to situations where the eyewitness only believed the perpetrator to have possessed a weapon. In addition, I know of at least one case where the defense pursued a weapon-focus type argument in connection with an incident of indecent exposure.

(3) Eyewitness Confidence: Eligible jurors tend to believe witnesses who are confident (Brigham & Bothwell, 1983; Cutler, Penrod, & Dexter, 1990; Lindsay, 1994; Wells et al., 1979; Whitley & Greenberg, 1986) and some judge's instructions reflect that confidence is an important factor to be considered when evaluating eyewitness evidence (*Neil v. Biggers,* 1972). Similarly, Rahaim and Brodsky (1982) found that 27 out of 42 practicing attorneys agreed with the proposition that very confident eyewitnesses are most likely to be correct. However, a meta-analysis of 35 laboratory and field experiments has shown that the correlation between eyewitness accuracy and confidence is typically weak, around +.25 (Bothwell, Deffenbacher, & Brigham, 1987).

With regard to face identification accuracy, several laboratory studies have shown a near zero correlation between witness confidence and accuracy (Deffenbacher, 1980; Hosch & Cooper, 1982; Hosch & Platz, 1988; Jenkins & Davies, 1985; Smith & Vela, 1992; Wells, 1993), while other studies have shown a modest correlation (Sporer, 1993), and some a significant correlation (Brigham, Maass, Snyder, & Spaulding, 1982; Read, 1995). At least two studies have shown that witnesses who are misled by an interviewer can be significantly more confident in identifications that are inaccurate than in ones that are accurate (Lindsay et al., 1981; Ryan & Geiselman, 1991). Furthermore, little correlation has been found between witnesses' predictions of future accuracy, such as "I could recognize him again" or "I got a good look at him," and the accuracy of their later identifications (Geiselman, Haghighi, & Stown, 1995; Haghighi & Geiselman, 1996; Sporer, 1992; Wells, 1984). Witness confidence, in most cases, also has failed to predict earwitness voice identification accuracy (Yarmey & Matthys, 1992).

A more recent meta-analysis of laboratory experiments by Sporer, Penrod, Read, and Cutler (1995) replicated the Bothwell et al. (1987) finding of a relatively weak confidence-accuracy correlation (+.29). When the analysis was confined to only those eyewitnesses who chose to identify someone, however, the correlation was somewhat greater, around +.40. Sporer et al. (1995) concluded that "the index that jurors ought to... rely upon should arguably vary as a function of the witness situation they confront: if the jury learns about the existence of choosing and non-choosing witnesses (who may be called by the defense) perhaps the overall confidence-accuracy relation is most relevant. If all the witnesses (or the only witness) are choosers, perhaps the confidence-accuracy for choosers is most relevant. ...The testimony should emphasize that confidence is far from a perfect indicator of witness accuracy." Even when the analysis is restricted to only those witnesses who choose someone, the correlation between stated confidence and the accuracy of their choices has not been reliably significant with live, staged events. Haghighi and Geiselman (1996), for example, found no predictive power of confidence in any of three experiments involving realistic classroom disruptions with hundreds of observers (all correlations less than +.21).

There is some evidence that a witness's confidence is highly correlated with identification accuracy only when the witness's opportunity for observing and remembering the perpetrator are ideal (Cutler & Penrod, 1989; Deffenbacher, 1980; Read, 1995). This "optimality" hypothesis states that witness confidence will discriminate accurate from inaccurate witnesses when the conditions for viewing and identifying a suspect should produce accurate identifications once the suspect is captured. For example, Cutler and Penrod (1989) found that confidence was more likely to predict identification accuracy when witnesses viewed a perpetrator without a disguise under good conditions as compared to with a disguise under poor conditions. Likewise, Read, Vokey, and Hammersley (1990) found the confidence-accuracy correlation to be lower when the perpetrator's appearance had changed over time.

There are several reasons why eyewitness confidence and accuracy are not correlated under many conditions. First, the act of making a choice itself appears to elevate the certainty of eyewitnesses for reasons that are independent of their accuracy (Leippe, 1980; Malpass & Devine, 1981), such as an inflated belief in their perceptual-memory abilities (Schulster, 1981). It also is known that people do have illusions of familiarity (Whittlesea, 1993) and repeatedly recalling something can increase their confidence in what they are thinking about, regardless of whether they are accurate or not (Kelley & Lindsay, 1993). Hastie, Landsman, and Loftus (1978) found witnesses who were questioned several times about an event became more confident about the accuracy of their recollections. Witnesses probably become more accepting of their responses and become committed to them with rehearsal over time. Read (1995) states that "in real-world forensic situations, criminal events are often followed by the witness/victim's personal thoughts and mental rehearsal, often at the encouragement and/or direction of investigative and legal personnel. By doing so, there is reason to believe that witnesses may come to overestimate their ability to identify someone by misattributing one kind of knowledge for another." Similarly, Wells, Ferguson, and Leippe (1981) found that witnesses who were briefed about the questions they might encounter on cross-examination and who were asked to think about their answers expressed more confidence in their identifications at trial.

Witnesses also become more confident in incorrect identifications if they are told that someone else has made the same identification (Luus, 1991; Luus & Wells, 1994). Finally, witnesses often show a high degree of confidence in information supplied by other persons, whether or not that information is accurate (Loftus, Donders, Hoffman, & Schooler, 1989). Leading suggestions, such as "So you are certain this is the man" or "That's our suspect" are likely to inflate a witness's confidence at trial. Thus, eyewitness confidence can be altered independently of eyewitness accuracy (Luus & Wells, 1994). In a case where I was asked to review the eyewitness evidence, the eyewitness stated that two persons in the photoarray resembled the assailant whom she remembered. The investigating officer said "Well choose one." She did and he replied "No, that's not him." In response, she replied "So it must be the other one," to which the officer stated "Yes, that's him." This experience must have affected the witness's confidence in her second selection, and she was very certain at the subsequent preliminary hearing and trial.

In sum, the experimental results are mixed at best, and the confidence expressed by an eyewitness should not be taken as an indication that the report of an eyewitness is accurate. Approximately half of the eligible jurors polled in one survey believed that confidence should be a good indicator of accuracy (Kassin & Barndollar, 1992). In two other surveys, laypersons ranked eyewitness confidence as the third and fourth most important factor in assessing the likelihood of eyewitness accuracy (Lindsay, 1994), falling behind only attention to the criminal and opportunity to view the criminal. It is clear that jurors rely heavily on the confidence expressed by an eyewitness, and they often do so to the exclusion of other evidence including other eyewitness factors known to adversely affect accuracy (Cutler et al., 1990; Lindsay et al., 1981). Luus and Wells (1994) conclude: "We have dire concerns about eyewitness confidence malleability in terms of what it might mean in actual criminal cases. Because the confidence that an eyewitness expresses in his or her identification has been sanctioned as a reliable cue to accuracy in judicial rulings (e.g., *Neil v. Biggers*, 1972) and because people intuitively use confidence to judge the likelihood of identification accuracy, we argue that there is an incentive for police and attorneys to manipulate their witness's confidence" (pp. 720-721).

(4) Cross-racial Identification: There is some laboratory evidence that same-race identifications tend to be more accurate than cross-race identifications (Brigham & Barkowitz, 1978; Barkowitz & Brigham, 1982; Chance, Goldstein, & McBride, 1975; Galper, 1973; Malpass & Kravitz, 1969; Teitelbaum & Geiselman, 1996), especially after a time delay up to seven weeks (Barkowitz & Brigham, 1982). Two meta-analyses of 14 and 18 laboratory studies (Bothwell et al., 1989; Shapiro & Penrod, 1986) and two more ecologically valid field studies (Brigham et al., 1982; Hosch & Platz, 1984) all confirmed the cross-race effect. The effect is typically a 10-to-15 percent difference in accurate same-race versus cross-race identifications. The effect has been studied most extensively for black versus Caucasian identifications, but the effect also has been found with other races as well such as Asians (Chance, Goldstein, & McBride, 1975; Luce, 1974; Ng & Lindsay, 1994; O'Toole, Deffenbacher, Valentin, & Abdi, 1994) and Hispanics (Geiselman et al., 1995). Malpass (1982) reviewed 16 studies on cross-racial identification and concluded that 15 of them showed the effect. A more recent meta-analysis of studies on cross-racial identification has confirmed the earlier findings (Anthony, Copper, & Mullen, 1992). A cross-race effect also has been observed on the quality of composites constructed by eyewitnesses (Ellis, Davies, & McMurran, 1979). In contrast to the research evidence, surveys indicate that as many as half of the eligible jurors polled do not appear to consider cross-racial identification to be a significant problem (Kassin & Barndollar, 1992; Loftus, 1979; Yarmey & Jones, 1983).

The cause of the cross-race effect is still in debate. There is no evidence that racial attitude plays any role (Brigham & Barkowitz, 1978), and the effect does not seem to be lesser for persons who say they have more frequent contact with the other race (Brigham & Barkowitz, 1978; Malpass & Kravitz, 1969; Ng & Lindsay, 1994). However, children found living in mixed-race environments sometimes show less of a cross-race effect on identification accuracy than children living in segregated environments (Ferman & Entwistle, 1976). Also, there is some evidence that adults who have close friends of the other race show less of a cross-race effect, suggesting that the quality of the exposure may make a difference (Lavrakas, Buri, and Mayzner, 1976; Lindsay & Wells, 1983). Shepherd and Deregowski (1981) have speculated that the cross-race effect occurs because people tend to differentially attend to persons of their own race. Anthony et al. (1992) have concluded that the effect is related to differences in the representations that group members hold of persons from other groups, which in turn affects how faces from same and other races are processed. What is known is that observers rely more on featural information from faces and less on the configural relationships between the features when making cross-race identifications (Rhodes, Tan, Brake, & Taylor, 1989); but attention to configural relationships produces more accurate face recognition (Wells & Hryciw, 1984). Thus, the natural perceptual behavior of people appears consistent with the negative cross-race effect.

It should be noted that not all studies have produced a complete cross-race effect (Ayuk, 1990), and some have not produced the effect at all (Lindsay & Wells, 1983). In fact, one might think that because faces of another race "look alike," the lineups used for cross-race identifications would be more fair than lineups used for same-race identifications (see factor 11 on lineup fairness). This could account for some of the discrepant outcomes in the literature (Egeth, 1995; Lindsay & Wells, 1983). However, even with forensically-relevant experimental procedures, cross-race identifications have been found to be less accurate than same-race identifications (see Geiselman et al., 1995).

(5) Expectations, Ethnic Biases, and Stereotypes: Stereotype-based expectancies affect information seeking, information processing, hypothesis formation, and judgments (Hamilton, Sherman, & Ruvolo, 1990). For example, there is some laboratory evidence that eyewitnesses from different ethnic backgrounds give different judgments of a perpetrator's height and weight. In particular, Asian witnesses have been found to recall both Asian and Caucasian perpetrators to be shorter and less heavy than Caucasian witnesses (Chen & Geiselman, 1993; Lee & Geiselman, 1994). Also, both Asian and Caucasian witnesses have been found to recall Asian perpetrators to be shorter and less heavy than Caucasian perpetrators who are actually the same height and weight. These ethnically-related biases and stereotypes should be taken into consideration by the trier of fact when evaluating the accuracy of eyewitness recollections of another person's height and weight.

Other research has shown stereotype-based expectancy effects on eyewitness recollections of the behavior of police (Boon & Davies, 1988) and of female drivers (Diges, 1988). Thus, there appears to be some merit in the observation of one early forensic psychologist that as eyewitnesses "we tend to see and hear what we expect to see and hear" (Whipple, 1918, p.

228). As Bruner, Postman, and Rodrigues (1951) put it: "Given less than optimal stimulus conditions, certain factors of past experience may play a determinative part in perceptual organization... The smaller the quantity of appropriate information, the greater the probability of an initial hypothesis being confirmed even if environmental events fail to agree with such hypotheses." As an illustration of this premise, Tickner and Poulton (1975) found police officers to "see" petty thefts that did not occur in a videotape of a street scene. In another experiment, Mantwill, Koehnken, and Aschermann (1995) found experienced blood donors to "recall" details of a videotaped blood donation that were not present in the video. Persons not familiar with donating blood did not show a high frequency of such errors. There also is a modest literature showing that people rely on stereotypes of appearance and criminality in making identifications from photoarrays and lineups (Bull & Green, 1980; Yarmey, 1994). In sum, beliefs can literally create reality (Snyder, 1984).

There also is laboratory evidence that persons who converse with eyewitnesses often interpret their reports in a stereotypical manner. For example, Allport and Postman (1958) showed observers a subway scene in which an African-American male was depicted as having a conversation with an agitated white male dressed in a worker's garb. The white man was gesturing and holding a razor. The observers viewed the scene and described it to other persons, who in turn told third persons, and so on, up to six persons, as in a "telephone game." In over half the groups, the final participant in the chain told a version in which the African-American was holding the razor rather than the white man. The researchers interpreted their findings in terms of the impact of cultural expectations on perceptions. It is important to note, however, that the Allport and Postman study bears only on the issue of distortions by others of the reports of eyewitnesses who had a clear view, rather than distortions by the primary eyewitnesses themselves at the time of the event (Treadway & McCloskey, 1987). An attempt to demonstrate an effect of racial stereotypes directly on the observers' perceptions failed with this experimental design (Treadway & McCloskey, 1989).

(6) Pressures to Choose: Some laboratory studies have shown that even when the perpetrator is not present in a photoarray, witnesses tend to select someone 30-93 percent of the time anyway (Buckhout, Alper, Chern, Silverberg, & Slomovits, 1974; Egan, Pittner, & Goldstein, 1977; Memon, Dionne, Short, Maralani, MacKinnon, & Geiselman, 1988; Sporer, 1993; Wells & Turtle, 1986; Yu & Geiselman, 1992). Standard admonishment instructions were read to the witnesses in most of these studies. High rates of false identifications also have been observed in staged-crime experiments that maintain the ruse of being actual or genuine criminal investigations (Foster et al., 1994; Malpass & Devine, 1980; Murray & Wells, 1982). In fact, rates of misidentification appear to be much lower in laboratory studies than in more realistic crime enactments (Lindsay & Harvie, 1988) while correct recognition rates appear to be appreciably higher in laboratory settings (Shapiro & Penrod, 1986). The rate with which actual victim/witnesses choose anyone from a photoarray or lineup drops dramatically, however, when a deadly weapon was involved in the crime (Tollestrup et al., 1994). This is presumably due to the effects of weapon focus at the time of the event (see factor 2).

There are several apparent reasons for the high rates of misidentification. First, witnesses often make relative judgments (which one looks the most like the perpetrator) rather than absolute judgments (Wells, 1984). If a witness is determined to make a selection, then a relative-judgment "identification" can be produced with any photoarray or lineup, whether the perpetrator is present or not. There is a fundamental difference between person recognition and person identification. The former refers to a sense of having seen the person before, or a feeling of familiarity, whereas the latter refers to knowing who someone is, or "he did it." There is evidence that witnesses who say at the time of the test that they chose the one who "looks the most like him" are less likely to be accurate than witnesses who say "I just recognize him" (Stern & Dunning, 1994).

Compliance pressures also can be especially strong in situations where ambiguity and authority are prominent (Cialdini, 1988), and this includes interactions with investigators for both the prosecution and the defense. There have been instances where investigators have flat out told the witness that the suspect is present in the array, and laboratory evidence has shown that such inappropriate statements produce false identifications (Paley & Geiselman, 1989). Subtle changes in the instructions given to the witness can profoundly affect the likelihood of a selection (Cutler et al., 1987; O'Rourke et al., 1989). Even with appropriate admonishments, witnesses are likely to infer on their own that someone in the array is the suspect (Koehnken & Maass, 1985; Nisbett & Ross, 1980; Wells, 1993). It is unlikely that the authorities would exert the effort, time, and cost of conducting the lineup unless they had good reasons (other evidence) to do so. Combining suggestive lineup instructions with a suggestive photoarray (see factor 11) has been found to increase false identifications by 20 percent (Buckhout, Figueroa, & Hoff, 1975).

In addition, an innocent person who matches the description of the perpetrator is likely to be falsely identified when placed in a photoarray or lineup where the alternatives do not match the description (Lindsay & Wells, 1980). In a field experiment, Read (1995) found that the longer witnesses had to view a "perpetrator," the more likely they were to make false identifications from perpetrator-absent photoarrays. Perhaps these witnesses felt they must recognize the perpetrator because they had a good view, and should recognize the person (Read, 1994). In fact, people are poor at predicting what they will or will not recollect or recognize at a later time (Koriat, 1994).

Finally, witnesses are more likely to choose someone if they are told that another witness chose someone (Luus, 1991). In one case that I reviewed, the husband failed to make an identification initially, but after an evening at home with his wife who had made an identification, he returned to the police station to make a positive identification of the suspect. To limit the impact of such cross contamination of witnesses who know one another, investigating officers should at a minimum change the position of the suspect from one administration of a photoarray to another.

The perceived consequences of making a selection do not appear to reduce the likelihood of a witness making a selection. In a laboratory study conducted by Foster et al. (1994), "witnesses" were shown a videotape depicting a simulated bank robbery and were asked to identify the robber from a photoarray. One group of participants was told that this was an actual crime and "Now the big question in court will be, 'Can an identification be made from this film?' We are here to help the court answer this question." Other participants were told that this was a simulated crime and this is a research experiment. Approximately 80 percent of the participants selected a photo of someone when the perpetrator was not present in the array, and this was the case regardless of the perceived consequences of their actions (p. 116).

There are some experimental results and court rulings indicating that single person "showups" are more likely to lead to false identifications than full photoarrays or lineups (Behrman & Vayder, 1994; Malpass & Devine, 1983; *Neil v. Biggers*, 1972; Wagenaar, 1992; Wells et al., 1979). False identifications would be expected especially under highly suggestive conditions because, with a bias to choose someone, the suspect is the only alternative. Suggestive contexts could include field identifications where the suspect is held by police, perhaps in handcuffs, or biasing statements made at the showup by authority figures. Thus, the caution about showups, especially under suggestive conditions, is justified and some judge's model instructions to the jury on eyewitness identification include a statement on the merits of a witness picking from a group of similar individuals (*U.S. v. Telfaire*, 1972). Nonetheless, Gonzalez, Ellsworth, and Pembroke (1993) found no difference between showups and full lineups in producing false identifications. These researchers concluded that under the conditions they created, the showups minimized the problem of relative-judgment identifications that often is found with full lineups. That is, with only one alternative, the witness cannot select "the best" or closest alternative, which may be in error. Wells (1993) has concluded that a lineup which contains only one person matching the verbal description(s) is probably more dangerous than a single-person showup, but a fair lineup is probably better than a single-person showup (p. 562).

There appear to be fewer false identifications with the sequential presentation of photographs rather than a simultaneous presentation (Cutler & Penrod, 1988; Lindsay, Lea, & Fulford, 1991; Lindsay & Wells, 1985; Sporer, 1994). Sequential presentation of photos promotes absolute judgments (comparing each photo to memory for the person) whereas simultaneous presentation promotes relative judgments (comparing photos to each other to select which one "best" resembles the person). The rate of correct identifications does not differ as a function of the type of presentation; there is no improvement for correct identifications with the sequential procedure over the standard procedure. It must be noted that the reduction of false identifications is achieved without allowing the witness to go back in the sequential case. If the witness is allowed to go back and make between-photo comparisons, the relative-judgment process would be the same as with simultaneous presentation and the rate of false positives could be the same (Lindsay et al., 1991). Also, if one photo stands out in some way, then sequential presentation should result in a bias to select that photo just as with simultaneous presentation.

Laboratory research indicates that quick positive identifications are more likely to be accurate than slow positive identifications and long no-identification responses tend to be more accurate than quick no-identification responses (Stern & Dunning, 1994; Sporer, 1993, 1994). With all other factors being equal and a fair photoarray or lineup (see factor 11), an immediate positive identification would appear to be more likely to be accurate than a slow selection on the order of several seconds or minutes. However, the relation between speed and accuracy is probably affected by social factors. Koehnken and Maass (1988), for example, found research participants to make extremely slow identifications when they were led to believe that their testimony would form part of a criminal investigation. Conversely, at live lineups, some witnesses may make a rapid selection to escape the aversiveness of the situation (Sporer, 1994).

(7) Influences from Postevent Sources: Numerous laboratory experiments have demonstrated that memory is an active, constructive process, where information received after an incident can markedly alter and otherwise distort the witness's original memory for the event (Belli, Windschitl, McCarthy, & Winfry, 1992; Christiaansen, Sweeney, & Ochalek, 1983; Fruzzetti, Toland, Teller, & Loftus, 1992; Loftus, 1979, 1992). There is some evidence that the original memory and the new information "blend" together to form an embellished composite memory (Loftus & Hoffman, 1989). The biasing information can include misleading photos or distorted facial composites (Jenkins & Davies, 1985), as well as leading or misleading verbal information presented to the witness during questioning (Loftus, Miller, & Burns, 1978; Loftus & Zanni, 1975) or in statements made by other witnesses (Loftus & Greene, 1980). At a photoarray or live lineup, for example, leading questions and statements such as "So you are certain this is the man" or "That's our suspect" can increase the likelihood that the witness

will continue to identify the same person in the future and with greater confidence.

Eyewitnesses also tend to rehash the event with others and in their own minds. In doing so, they may unconsciously fill in gaps and details and alter memory so that their memories conform to information learned about the incident after the incident. In this way, the witness satisfies a normal psychological need to reduce uncertainty and does so by eliminating conflicts and inconsistencies between information in memory and other information acquired later (Bem, 1967). The act of verbally rehashing a witnessed event has been found to lead to poorer face identification performance (Schooler & Engstler-Schooler, 1990), and it also can lead to further alterations in memory subsequent to the first identification. Consider the following case where I served as an eyewitness expert. A lone eyewitness to a killing identified a suspect from a photoarray, but told investigators that he thought he saw this person on an earlier occasion in his neighborhood, not at the killing (see factor 8 on unconscious transference). By the time of the preliminary hearing, however, the witness now believed with great certainty that the person whom he had recognized earlier in the photoarray was in fact the killer. While the change of testimony was explained by the witness as an earlier "fear response" against identifying the perpetrator, the pattern of carry-over effects and increased confidence is characteristic of participants in laboratory experiments who are mistaken. Eyewitness expert testimony was relevant in this case.

Distortions of eyewitness accounts also have been observed when witnesses cross-talk with other persons (Allport & Postman, 1958). Hollin and Clifford (1983) found that laboratory eyewitnesses changed their original reports to bring themselves into agreement with the recall of other witnesses based on a group discussion. Similarly, observers to a more realistic pocketbook theft were observed to fabricate details under group pressure (Alper, Buckhout, Chern, Harwood, & Slomovits, 1976). While another experiment found no effect of such group discussions on lineup identification performance (Rupp, Warmbrand, Karash, & Buckhout, 1976), the U.S. Supreme Court requires that witnesses make an identification that has an "independent basis" in perception (Levine & Tapp, 1973). Consider the following case example where I was asked to attend a live lineup procedure on behalf of a defendant charged with multiple counts of armed robbery. There were several witnesses from different incidents who were transported to Men's Central Jail together in vans. At the lineup staging area, the group was properly admonished by the supervising Deputy to refrain from interacting with the other witnesses in any way during the lineup. They also were encouraged to walk on stage to have a better view, but to not stop in front of any one member of the lineup. Both of the Deputy's instructions were violated. One witness muttered "That's him," other witnesses nudged one another, and others became stationary on stage before the defendant while the others looked on. Given that some counts were minor and some more serious, this cross contamination created a dangerous situation that was likely to cause a bias to make a selection, heightened confidence in the selection, and a carry-over effect to a positive in-court identification (see factors 3, 6, & 9), thus requiring expert testimony. Even without any contamination between the witnesses, any flaws in the particular lineup that was constructed would affect the identifications of all the witness (see factor 11). Wells et al. (1994) recommend that different lineups be constructed for each eyewitness.

The content and phrasing of questions by investigators also can affect what a witness believes to be true. For example, witnesses will give higher estimates of vehicle speed when the question contains "smashed" rather than "hit" (Loftus & Palmer, 1974) and witnesses will remember a yield sign as being a stop sign if "stop sign" is inserted into a question about something else (Loftus et al., 1978). Estimates of age can be affected by an interviewer's reference to the "man" versus the "young man," and estimates of weight can be similarly affected by an interviewer's reference to the suspect's occupation (Christiaansen et al., 1983). A useful illustration of this phenomenon that can be used with jurors in court is a study showing that mock jurors have difficulty remembering what a witness actually said in court versus what an attorney implied in his questioning of the witness (Holst & Pezdek, 1992). Some eyewitnesses come to firmly believe that the misleading suggestions by others are "real" memories and they loose track of the actual source of the information (Zaragoza & Lane, 1994).

The biasing effects of post-event information typically are substantial, decreasing accurate recall performance by as much as 20 to 30 percent (Lindsay, 1993). In some cases, misleading post-event information has been found to negatively affect the recollections of over half the witnesses (Geiselman, Fisher, Cohen, Surtes, & Holland, 1986). In contrast, Yuille and Cutshall (1986) were unable to confuse actual witnesses to a violent crime with misleading questioning. The misleading effects are more likely to be observed with peripheral details than central features of events (Loftus, 1979) and they are more likely to be observed after delays on the order of days rather than minutes (Belli et al., 1992). They also are more likely to be observed when the source of the information is thought to be reliable (Dodd & Bradshaw, 1980; Smith & Ellsworth, 1987), such as an authority figure. Thus, there is some debate as to whether the effect is really a distortion of memory or whether the effect reflects social pressures on the witness (McCloskey & Zaragoza, 1985). Nevertheless, there is little debate as to the potential contamination of eyewitness reports from post-event sources or that eyewitnesses come to firmly believe that the suggested memories are real (Weingardt, Toland, & Loftus, 1994).

(8) Unconscious Transference: It would seem logical that prior exposure to a person would enable a witness to be in a better position to identify that person if seen at a crime event. However, the phenomenon of "unconscious transference" is said to occur when a witness "remembers" another person as having been at a crime location or as having played a certain role at the crime event when in fact the witness actually saw the person under circumstances other than that being described by the witness (Buckhout, 1974; Houts, 1956; Loftus, 1976; Read, Tollestrup, Hammersley, McFadzen, & Christensen, 1990; Ross, Ceci, Dunning, & Toglia, 1994). It is possible that the feeling of familiarity caused by the prior exposure would lead a witness to honestly make a false identification. Moreover, the act of making the identification would then lead the witness to become certain of the selection (see factor 3). Unconscious transference can occur when the perpetrator looks similar to someone who the witness has known or has seen in the neighborhood prior to the incident (Houts, 1956; Loftus, 1976; Wall, 1965). Even when an eyewitness consciously remembers hav-

ing seen both the bystander and the perpetrator, the witness can infer that the two are the same person (Loftus et al., 1989; Ross et al, 1994).

Houts (1956) describes an actual incident where a newspaper vendor mistakenly identified a sailor as the person who robbed him, when in fact the sailor had been only a frequent customer on prior occasions, and was on board a ship when the robbery took place. Other, more recent real-world cases of unconscious transference have been documented (e.g., Buckhout, 1984). In laboratory experiments, significant numbers of witnesses have identified persons from lineups whose faces had appeared only in a book of mugshots that they had viewed one week earlier, not at the crime scene (Brown, Deffenbacher, & Sturgill, 1977; Davies, Shepherd, & Ellis, 1979). In another series of laboratory experiments, eyewitnesses were found to be three times more likely to mistakenly identify a bystander to a staged event as the perpetrator than observers who were not exposed to the bystander (Ross et al., 1994). Similarly, Buckhout (1974) found 40 percent of students in a classroom to identify a bystander to a staged assault on their professor. In yet another staged experiment (Brown et al., 1977), an innocent bystander whose mugshot was seen in a preliminary array was as likely to be identified in a subsequent lineup as the criminal whose mugshot was not shown previously. This finding led the researchers to conclude that "we would tend to distrust indictments in situations such as those where witnesses had previously seen the suspects' mug shots" (p. 316).

There also is some laboratory evidence that witnesses show transference of perpetrator roles in identifications from photoarrays. In cases that involve multiple perpetrators, some witnesses show confusion as to which perpetrator carried out which actions during a crime (Geiselman, MacArthur, & Meerovitch, 1993). In that experiment, witnesses showed a strong bias to label any person they identified as having been the principal assailant.

Demonstrations of a dissociation between feelings of recognition and awareness of the source of that familiarity are common in observers (Johnson & Raye, 1981). There is considerable debate, however, as to whether this phenomenon is truly unconscious or whether it is caused by a conscious inference that a person who seems to be familiar is the person who committed the crime (Geiselman et al., 1993; Ross et al., 1994). In either case, however, a false identification is made. It also should be noted that some researchers have found the phenomenon to be difficult to demonstrate experimentally (Read et al., 1990) and they believe that unconscious transference may be a rare, but possible, event.

When asked to clarify unconscious transference with an example during testimony, I have related the following true incident from my personal experience. As I was walking near my residence in the early morning, I passed an unkempt young man sitting on some stairs without a shirt. He appeared not to belong in the neighborhood and he stared at me with what I believed to be a menacing look. Upon returning toward my residence, I observed a police cruiser with lights flashing and two officers hand-cuffing an unkempt young male with no shirt. The man appeared to be the same person whom I had seen earlier, and I believed the man to be the same person. As I walked further, the man I had seen earlier was still sitting on the stairs. Had the circumstances been different, one can easily understand how I could have mistakenly identified the wrong person as an eyewitness in a police investigation.

A second compelling anecdotal example involved another cognitive psychologist and barrister, Donald Thomson, who himself was mistakenly identified by a rape victim as the perpetrator. Professor Thomson seemed familiar to the victim because the professor was on a television show that she had been watching at the time. She was correct that he was familiar, but misattributed the source of the familiarity to the rape. Luckily for Professor Thomson, the show was live, which gave him a good alibi. The problem is that a person may seem familiar for the wrong reasons, and the witness may misattribute the source of the familiarity to the past incident.

(9) Carry-Over Effects: Witnesses often are asked to make an identification of a suspect a second or third time after viewing a single photo, a six-pack photoarray, or a live lineup containing the suspect. The consistency of these subsequent identifications, which include in-court identifications, commonly is taken as an indicator of witness reliability. However, it has been shown in experimental research that persons not present at an event, but viewed by witnesses in a single "showup" photo or in a six-pack photoarray, are later mistakenly selected as having been present at the event (Behrman & Vayder, 1994; Brown et al., 1977; Davies, Shepherd, & Ellis, 1979; Doob & Kirschenbaum, 1973; Gorenstein & Ellsworth, 1980). Viewing a large number of mugshots also has been found to reduce eyewitness accuracy in later identifying a suspect (Brigham & Cairns, 1988) due to the carry over of false identifications of persons contained in the mugshots. The consistent misidentification of the same person is commonly referred to as the "freezing" ef-

fect (Loftus, 1979). Despite the laboratory demonstrations of carry-over effects, the court ruled in *People v. Wimberly* (1992) that it was reasonable for police to use the defendant's photo in two different photoarrays with the same victim, and then carry out a live lineup.

The following case where I served as the expert serves to illustrate carry-over effects. A victim of an armed robbery returned to the crime scene the next day and found a personal identification card lying a few feet from where his own wallet had been found. The victim took the card to the police and told them that the person on the card was the perpetrator. One week later, the investigating officer placed the same photo in a six-pack array and showed the array to the victim who again positively identified the suspect. The victim further positively identified the defendant in court four months later after his arrest on a different matter. The suggestive nature of the victim's first post-crime exposure to the suspect, coupled with the possibility of carry-over effects and the modification of confidence with re-exposure, constituted the focus of my testimony at trial.

It appears that eyewitnesses are prone to misidentify the same person again when subsequently shown the actual perpetrator as an alternative to the wrongfully accused. This "commitment effect" could result from a perceived social pressure to be consistent (Festinger & Carlsmith, 1959; Wells, 1984) and/or an enhanced familiarity for the wrongfully accused person due to the prior identification (Brigham & Cairns, 1988; Gorenstein & Ellsworth, 1980). An eyewitness's beliefs about the accuracy of an identification may persist even when the identification has been called into question. This is because, in thinking about discredited beliefs, people tend to develop additional cognitive support for them that is outside the scope of the discrediting (Anderson, Lepper, & Ross, 1980).

In-court identifications are subject to both carry-over effects and the suggestiveness of the circumstances under which they are conducted. Because of these potentially biasing influences, I believe that in-court identifications are diagnostic only when the witness fails to make an identification of the defendant as the perpetrator. Two counsels have told me, however, of cases where eyewitnesses have pointed to persons other than the defendant in the courtroom, one was a spectator in the third row and the other was the defense attorney himself. The U.S. Supreme Court has recognized the danger of in-court show-ups (*Moore v. Illinois*, 1977), with particular notice by the courts when the accused is of a race different from anyone else in the courtroom (*U.S. v. Archibald,* 1984).

As described above, the typical sequence for a witness is to continue to select the same person across different identification mediums (photoarrays, live lineups, in-court identifications). However, on occasion, a witness will make a positive identification of a suspect from a photoarray and then fail to identify the same person at a live lineup. In some cases, the witness will identify someone else at the live lineup after having identified the suspect from a photoarray. When this happens, the defense will argue that the original identification was in error, whereas the prosecution will argue that considerable time has passed or that the suspect now looks different. It has been observed in laboratory experiments that identification accuracy does decline with time delay (Deffenbacher, 1986) as does memory for faces (Egan et al., 1977), and distortions of appearance from initial exposure to test do affect identification accuracy (Cutler & Penrod, 1989; Shapiro & Penrod, 1986; Terry, 1994). Conversely, sometimes a witness will fail to identify a suspect from a photoarray, but will positively identify the suspect from a live lineup. When this happens, the defense should argue that there are carry-over effects from the witness's viewing the suspect in the photoarray, whereas the prosecution will argue that the additional body cues enabled the witness to now identify the suspect.

Directly relevant to the evaluation of both of these dilemmas is the available research on the reliability of eyewitness identifications from different test media. Cutler, Berman, Penrod, and Fisher (1994) conducted a meta-analysis of approximately 20 laboratory experiments which examined the accuracy of eyewitness identifications from different test media. The test media ranged from live lineups, where the persons were required to walk around and speak, to still photos, where the persons were depicted in head and shoulder front profiles. Across studies, live lineups produced no more identifications of the actual perpetrator than photoarrays when he was included in the test media, but live lineups did produce approximately 20 percent fewer false identifications when he was not included in the test media. Thus, photoarrays produced significantly more mistaken identifications than live lineups, and live lineups did not serve to increase accurate identifications when the actual perpetrator was included in a live lineup.

Because of the observed variability among studies on test media, however, Cutler et al. (1994) stated that the conservative conclusion is that "there is no reason to believe that live lineups, video-taped lineups, or photoarrays produce substantial differences in identification performance" (p. 181). MacLeod,

Frowley, & Shepherd (1994) also have concluded that "although gender and familiar others can be recognized on the basis of movement information alone, it is unclear whether it plays any part in recognizing unfamiliar others save those who have unusual gaits or deformities" (p. 129). This is not to imply that a witness could never benefit from the extra bodily and speech cues available at a live lineup in any specific case, but rather that placing great weight on such cues when evaluating eyewitness identification testimony appears to be ill-advised. In sum, when a witness selects the police suspect from a live lineup having failed to identify the suspect from a photoarray, the possibility of carry-over effects must be seriously considered. When a witness fails to select the police suspect from a live lineup having already identified the suspect from a photoarray, the possibility must be considered that the original identification was in error. In such cases, the relevant issues can be presented in expert testimony to enable the trier of fact to arrive at a more informed evaluation of the eyewitness evidence.

(10) Forming Composite Facial Images: The intended purpose of any composite facial image is to narrow the range of potential suspects (e.g., race, hairstyle, facial hair, disfigurements) and to eliminate large sections of the population (Domingo, 1984). Using composite images to isolate a specific individual usually is not the intended goal, and experimental tests have shown only limited success in using composites to identify specific persons (Green & Geiselman, 1989). Where success was observed, the witness was able to form a good likeness of the perpetrator from memory immediately after viewing the person. At a minimum, an identification based on the viewing a composite image should not be taken as conclu-

sive evidence that the suspect and the perpetrator are one and the same person.

Hall (1976) and Hall and Ostrom (1975) conducted research in which observers viewed a person whom they later tried to identify from a live lineup. Some observers worked with a sketch artist to form a composite image prior to attempting to make an identification, whereas other observers simply waited a comparable amount of time. The results showed that those observers who participated in working with a sketch artist made more errors in their later identifications. One explanation for this result is that forcing the eyewitness to verbalize the constituent parts of a face with the artist causes the eyewitness to muddle his/her original memory for the face (Clifford & Davies, 1989), and therefore to distort his/her identification to be more in line with the sketch rather than the original memory. There is considerable evidence that the accuracy of a witness's verbal description of a face bears little relation to the witness's later accuracy of identification (Deffenbacher, 1991; Pigott & Brigham, 1985; Wells, 1985).

Negative carry-over effects also have been observed with eyewitnesses who are asked to work with a computer to generate a composite facial image of a perpetrator. One forensic psychologist commented, "We have discovered that after working with the computer, the subjects have a much more difficult time articulating a verbal description, and exhibit highly-anxious and indecisive reactions to photo lineups. ...this seems to adversely affect the subjects later ability to regenerate the cognitive image for comparison to either the photo lineup or live identification" (Psychology & Law E-mail Network, August 30, 1995).

In contrast, a negative carry-over effect does not appear to occur following work with one of the mechanical composite systems such as the Identi-kit (Mauldin & Laughery, 1981; Yu & Geiselman, 1993) unless the face of an innocent suspect closely resembles distortions made in the witness's composite of the actual perpetrator (Comish, 1987). In that case, the witness is likely to identify the innocent suspect as the perpetrator (Jenkins & Davies, 1985). In either case, the person who is ultimately arrested is likely to resemble the composite image. Therefore, the fact that a suspect resembles a composite should not be taken as conclusive evidence that the suspect and the perpetrator are one and the same person.

(11) Lineup and Photoarray Fairness: Given the bias to select someone from a group (see factor 6 above), the question then becomes why did the witness(es) select the defendant?

Aside from the possibility that the defendant was the perpetrator of the crime, any characteristic that would limit the eyewitness's selection of choices can be said to decrease the fairness of the lineup or photoarray. In effect, the functional size of an array of alternatives is reduced when it is biased and in some cases the functional size can be reduced to one. This happens when the verbal descriptions given by the eyewitnesses match only one person presented as an alternative (i.e., the suspect). With photoarrays or lineups that are not fair, several witnesses may all be in error because they are all drawn to the same biasing characteristic. Lindsay (1994) has complied a review of biased lineup procedures and their sources which include ignorance, sloppiness, and intentional bias.

Eyewitness expert testimony is especially useful in cases involving biased photoarrays because, unlike with a live lineup, the U.S. Supreme Court has ruled that a suspect or defendant has no right for counsel to be present when a photoarray is shown to eyewitnesses (*U.S. v. Ash*, 1973; see also *Kirby v. Illinois*, 1972). Counsel therefore has no opportunity to raise objections at the time of the procedure, and must move in a pretrial motion to suppress the identification with the expert's supporting declaration or testimony (see *Manson v. Brathwaite*, 1977). When denied such a motion, the expert's testimony is needed at trial. Given that unfair lineup procedures are poorly understood by judges and jurors (Lindsay, 1994), and given the limitations placed on such testimony by some trial judges (see Chapter 3), the expert and attorney must be prepared for a variety of question formats to expose the biased aspects of a photoarray or lineup.

Laboratory research has shown that simply placing one photo in an array at a slight angle can bias witnesses to select that photo (Buckhout, Figueroa, & Hoff, 1975). The angle cue seems more subtle than most elements that might bias witnesses to select a suspect from a photoarray or live lineup. Other research has shown more false identifications to faces matching the verbal description given by a witness than to faces not matching the verbal description, as well as more false identifications of persons wearing clothes similar to those worn by the perpetrator (Lindsay, Nosworthy, Martin, & Martynuck, 1994).

Constructing arrays that are fair can be difficult depending on the specific characteristics of the suspect and on the resources of the law-enforcement agency. Nevertheless, there are instances where problems of fairness require serious consideration. In one case that I examined, the defendant's moniker was "green eyes" and his photo was the only one that did not portray brown eyes. In another case, the defendant's photo was overexposed relative to the other photos and the witnesses had described the perpetrator as a "light-skinned black." In another case, the defendant was given a cigarette immediately before a live lineup and the witnesses had described the perpetrator as smelling of cigarette smoke. Ellison and Buckhout (1981), Loftus and Ketcham (1991) and Sobel (1984) all have described cases where the biasing elements were even more blatant, such as placing a black suspect in a lineup with five white persons. The problem of lineup fairness is sometimes compounded in that a cross-race effect has been found in investigators' ability to construct fair lineups (Brigham & Ready, 1985). Specifically, lineups of black males that are constructed by Caucasian officers show greater variability among the persons included than lineups of white males, and vice versa.

Bailey and Rothblatt (1985) describe the celebrated case of black activist Angela Davis, where a set of nine photographs contained three pictures of the defendant taken at an outdoor rally, two police mug shots of other women with their names displayed, a picture of a 55-year-old woman, and so on. In the lawyers' opinion, the choices were reduced to four pictures, three of which were of Davis. Thus, the probability of an eyewitness guessing the defendant was 75 percent.

To verify suspected bias, lineup or photoarray fairness can be evaluated to satisfy the expert or counsel with a simple test (Doob & Kirshenbaum, 1973; Wells et al., 1979; Wells, 1988). Persons who have no knowledge of this case and act independently should be given the verbal descriptions provided by the eyewitnesses in the case. They then should be shown the lineup or photoarray and be asked to select the person who best matches the descriptions. If the suspect is selected by more persons than would be expected by mere guessing (one-sixth of the persons if there are six alternatives in the array) and the persons in the other positions are selected less frequently, then the possibility of a biased lineup should be taken into consideration when considering the reliability of identifications made by the actual witnesses. Some psychologists have suggested that standards should be adopted for evaluating photoarrays and lineups for fairness and that an index of fairness should be derived for the test media used in any particular case (Brigham & Pfeifer, 1994). Law-enforcement investigators should head-off defense attacks on photoarray fairness by showing their own arrays in advance to other officers who know nothing about the case. The participants should be asked to select the suspect based on the verbal descriptions and to otherwise look for bias in the arrays. Tollestrup et al. (1994) found some officers in their field study who routinely follow such procedures prior to showing an array to an actual eyewitness in a case.

In general, the non-suspect alternatives in an array should be selected based on their match to the verbal descriptions given by the eyewitnesses. Selection of the alternatives should not be based on their visual similarity to the suspect alone because this may result in the suspect appearing as a composite of the features shared by the others. This could artificially cause the suspect to stand out as the most desirable alternative even if an eyewitness is guessing (Navon, 1992). However, a special problem arises when the verbal descriptions provided by the witnesses are vague or do not match the appearance of the suspect. Placing five photos of persons who all match the verbal descriptions in an array with a suspect who appears different would cause the suspect to stand out and perhaps be selected on that basis alone (Lindsay et al., 1994). I have served as an expert on several cases where the suspect's race did not match the race given by the witness(es) in their verbal statements. This would be expected with some mixed-race individuals, but the contrast in other cases has been striking. Such discrepancies call into question the validity of the suspect's culpability (Pigott & Brigham, 1985; Sporer, 1992; Wells, 1985). In the more gray-area cases, investigators should put together one array of six persons who reasonably fit the verbal descriptions (card "A"), and a second array consisting of the suspect along with five alternatives that visually resemble the suspect without grossly deviating from the verbal descriptions any more than necessary (card "B"). The identification procedure should then proceed with the witness viewing card "A" under the standard admonishment, followed by card "B," also under the standard admonishment. This procedure not only addresses the problem of the description-appearance discrepancy, but it also allows for a "blank," no-suspect array to precede the suspect-present array. Wells (1984) has shown that this sequence reduces the likelihood of a false identification on the suspect-present array.

Multiple-suspect photoarrays or lineups pose multiple problems for evaluating the weight of an identification made by an eyewitness and therefore, they should be avoided (Wells, 1988; Wells et al., 1994). Lineups with one suspect and several innocent persons have been found to reduce misidentifications relative to multiple-suspect lineups (Wells & Turtle, 1986). First, the functional size of a lineup is reduced for any one suspect in a multiple-suspect lineup should the eyewitness recognize one of the other suspects. This situation increases the likelihood that the witness will select the remaining suspects by guessing. Such guessing is likely to be more probable given an inflated sense of confidence caused by the witness's identification of the other person in the lineup. The act of making a selection is known to increase witness confidence (Leippe, 1980; Malpass & Devine, 1981). Thus, the only useful investigative purpose of multiple-suspect photoarrays would be to narrow the number of potential suspects with one eyewitness, and then to construct individual, single-suspect arrays to be shown to other witnesses (Wells & Turtle, 1986).

With multiple suspects in a multiple-perpetrator crime, constructing separate photoarrays for the suspects will solve some of the problems, but not necessarily all of them. I served as an expert on a case where there were three suspects arrested together. Photos of the suspects were placed in separate arrays and the five alternatives in each array were all different photos. Unfortunately, the background in all of the alternative photos was light gray whereas the background in each of the three suspect photos was black. Each witness in the case was shown all three arrays, such that the suspects' photos were likely to stand out not only because of the discrepant backgrounds, but also because of the consistent discrepancy across all three arrays. This would likely compound the problem of bias. Consistent with this possibility, the witnesses almost uniformly selected all suspects in the photoarrays, but failed to identify any of them one month later from three separate and fair, live lineups.

An issue related to fairness is the transformation of appearance of a defendant at a live lineup from that which existed on the day of the event. Shapiro and Penrod (1986) found significant negative effects on the recognizability of suspects in controlled laboratory experiments with relatively simple changes in the perpetrator, such as a hat covering the hair or a change in hairstyle. Terry (1994) found similar results with the addition of a beard. This can lead to either a failure to identify the perpetrator or a mistaken identification of someone else. Upper parts of a face appear to be most important in recognition (Davies, Ellis, & Shepherd, 1981), such that a hat and sunglasses form a more problematic disguise than the stereotypical bandanna around the nose and mouth.

(12) Multiple Perpetrators: There is some laboratory evidence that identification accuracy concerning any one perpetrator decreases as the number of perpetrators having taken part in an event increases (Clifford & Hollin, 1981). When attention is divided or is switched back and forth between two or more targets, subsequent identification performance is less accurate (Kahneman, 1975). There also is a possibility that a witness will "blend" the characteristics of multiple perpetrators into a composite image (Loftus & Hoffman, 1989). I have seen the defense use this argument to suggest a mistaken identification, and I have seen the prosecution use this argument to explain why a witness's verbal description of a primary suspect contains characteristics of another person believed to have been present. As noted with factor 8, there also is the potential for witnesses to confuse the roles played by different perpetrators in multiple perpetrator crimes (Geiselman et al., 1993).

(13) Who Remembers Best?: One might believe that persons who routinely interact with the public make better eyewitnesses. However, field studies of convenience store cashiers have found them to be less than 50% accurate in identifying persons whom they encountered as customers two-hours earlier

counting out 100 pennies (Brigham et al., 1982; Platz & Hosch, 1988). Similar findings were reported by Krafka and Penrod (1985), who also observed nearly one-third of the clerks to mistakenly select someone from a photoarray when the "customer" was not included. Of course, these persons did not commit a crime in the store such that attention would be drawn to them as suspected criminals. There is some evidence that a perceived criminal act "catches witnesses' attention such that they encode more information about the thief than they do if the person interacts with them, but does not do anything unusual" (Hosch & Cooper, 1982, p. 651). However, studies on the effects of significant stress, as would be expected in the case of an armed robbery, suggest that performance would be further impaired in these studies under more stressful conditions (Bothwell & Hosch, 1987).

With a more salient event, Pigott et al. (1990) found the eyewitness accuracy of bank tellers to be similar to that of the clerks. In their experiment, a research assistant attempted to cash an altered check and argued with a teller for 90 seconds. Four to five hours later, another research assistant posing as a police officer showed the teller a photoarray that either included the "customer" or not. As with the clerks, less than half of the tellers correctly identified the person with whom they had argued and over one-third of the tellers mistakenly identified another person when the "customer" was not included in the array. It is interesting that most of the tellers in the study reported having had some training in being an eyewitness. A direct test of trained and untrained eyewitnesses produced no difference in subsequent eyewitness accuracy (Woodhead, Baddeley, & Simmonds, 1979).

Recent studies by Read et al. (1990) and Read (1995) have found the identification accuracy of convenience store and retail clerks to range from 38 to 75 percent (Read et al., 1990). In some of these studies, the "perpetrator" carried on a conversation with the clerk for as much as 12 minutes. Thus, the accuracy of the identifications appears to depend somewhat on the eyewitnessing conditions created in the specific experiments including the length of quality exposure time.

One might also believe that peace officers would make better eyewitnesses because of their interactions with the public. In fact, some surveys show that as many as 60 percent of eligible jurors believe that police officers do make better eyewitnesses (Kassin & Barndollar, 1992; Loftus, 1980). However, police academies rarely give any training on perceptual and memory concerns (Yarmey, 1986) and there is no evidence that training people to be better witnesses has any effect on performance (Loftus, 1979). At present, all studies but one with Canadian police (Yuille, 1984) have shown law-enforcement personnel to be no better witnesses than laypersons (Ainsworth, 1981). This is despite the opinions of many laypersons that police do make better witnesses. In fact, some studies have shown police to "see" crimes that did not take place (Clifford, 1976). Tickner & Poulton (1975) showed a camera panning a city scene that revealed some petty thefts. Police were equal to others in the detection of actual crimes, but police made more false accusations of crimes. Loftus, Levidow, and Duensing (1992) tested people's memory for things that went on at a visit to the Exploratorium in San Francisco including a simulated armed robbery. The average accuracy score was 74% for all visitors, but was 68% for law-enforcement personnel. Again, police were no more accurate than other people.

I have testified in several trials where the opposing counsel attempted to bolster the credibility of an eyewitness by pointing out the level of detail in the eyewitness's account. There is some evidence that jurors believe that persons who remember lots of detail are more reliable witnesses, and conversely, that the testimony of witnesses with poor memory for peripheral detail should be discounted (Lindsay, 1994). However, it appears from research studies that witnesses who have better memories for peripheral detail often fail to identify a perpetrator accurately (Cutler et al., 1987; Wells & Leippe, 1981). Similarly, Brigham et al. (1982) found in their field study of convenience store clerks that those who could identify one "customer" were no more likely to recognize another than clerks who could not identify the first.

In sum, it is difficult to predict from the available studies who will make a good eyewitness based on their occupation or the detail of their account. Neither intelligence nor verbal/spatial abilities, as measured by standardized tests, predict eyewitness ability (Brown et al., 1977; Powers, Andriks, & Loftus, 1979), and neither does a person's "cognitive style" for processing information (Christiaansen, Ochalek, & Sweeney, 1984) or a witness's own perceived face memory skills (Woodhead et al., 1979). With few exceptions, personality variables and personal views on crime-related issues also have been shown to have little power to predict face recognition or event recall (Clifford & Scott, 1978; Deffenbacher, Brown, & Sturgill, 1978; Geiselman et al., 1995; Haghighi & Geiselman, 1996). This provides further justification for the eyewitness expert to refrain from interviewing the eyewitnesses in any given case; there are no standard set of questions that the expert could ask an eyewitness to form an opinion.

One possible exception is a social-personality construct called "self monitoring" (Hosch, 1994; Hosch & Platz, 1984). High self monitors are persons who are constantly monitoring the people around them so as to determine how they themselves should appear and behave. If someone is constantly observing other people, there is a chance that they will have the opportunity to observe things that others may not. Even this effect is not strong (Geiselman et al., 1995) and is likely to be overshadowed by other factors in most cases (Haghighi & Geiselman, 1966).

Relevant to the question of "who remembers best" is the study of children and the elderly as eyewitnesses. My interpretation of the burgeoning volume of studies on children as witnesses is that children can be hypersuggestible when questioned improperly without adequate preparation (Ceci & Bruck, 1993). While children typically offer less complete reports than adults but their reports typically are no less accurate than those from adults (Saywitz & Geiselman, in press). With respect to person identification, there is evidence that fourth graders are less accurate than either eighth or eleventh graders in selecting a perpetrator from a photoarray (Brigham, Van Verst, & Bothwell, 1986). There are several available volumes on children as witnesses including Children's eyewitness memory (Ceci, Toglia, & Ross, 1987), Perspectives on children's testimony (Ceci, Ross, & Toglia, 1989), and Child victims, child witnesses (Goodman & Bottoms, 1993).

With respect to the elderly, there is some research which appears to show that they remember less information about events and that they remember less accurately than younger adults (List, 1986; Yarmey & Kent, 1980). Loftus et al. (1992) also found that older adults were more often misled by misleading postevent information. However, Yarmey and Kent (1980) found no difference in the accuracy of lineup identifications made by young and elderly adults. When interviewed properly, instead of in an artificial way, even the age-related difference in the amount of detail recalled has been eliminated with accuracy rates as high as 90 percent under certain circumstances (Mello & Fisher, 1995). Scogin et al. (1994) concluded that "age alone does not determine eyewitness competence."

8

Menu of Direct Examination Questions

This chapter presents suggested questions for direct examination of the eyewitness expert. The initial questions are to establish the credibility of the expert, followed by a question to elicit a general narrative on eyewitness information processing, followed in turn by substantive questions to present expert testimony on the factors from Chapter 7 that are relevant to the case at hand.

Establishing the Expert's Credentials

The following are sample questions and their inclusion will depend on the background of the particular expert. If the opposing counsel in a jury trial should interrupt this phase of questioning to stipulate as to the expert's credentials, the retaining attorney should move to continue this questioning anyway. To do otherwise, would interfere with the expert's ability to develop rapport with the jury. The jury wants to know something about the expert.

A. What is your occupation?
B. How long have you held that position?
C. What is your background in terms of education and training?
D. What is your current field of specialty?

E. Is this a recognized field of study within psychology? [Division 41 of the American Psychological Association is devoted to Psychology and Law, which includes a large number of scientists conducting research in eyewitness psychology.]

F. Have you conducted research in the area of eyewitness recollection?

G. Have you published any articles in the area of eyewitness identification?

H. What kinds of studies have you done (or have been done) in the area of eyewitness recollection? [This question pertains to general methodology. The advantages and limitations of both laboratory and field studies should be presented as part of the answer - see Chapter 5.]

I. Have you ever provided your expertise for law enforcement? [These activities include consultant roles on actual cases, as well as talks and workshops.]

J. Have you ever provided your expertise for the prosecution (or the defense)? [These activities would include "behind the scenes" preparation of cases in addition to providing testimony.]

K. Have you ever given expert testimony on eyewitness matters in court?

The Narrative on Eyewitness Information Processing

Many laypersons will believe that memory operates like a videotape that can be replayed later with great accuracy. The expert can challenge this belief by stating that a memory is an interpretation of the information that is acquired through the senses, rather than a faithful record. The expert can discuss the factors that are known to influence memory at each of the three stages of eyewitness information processing that were described in Chapter 7. Finally, the expert can point out the fragile and vulnerable nature of the mental processes involved at each stage. This narrative can be elicited with a general question such as the following:

L. Can you describe what is generally believed to occur in memory in an eyewitness situation? [Here reference is made to the brevity of the event, its emotional nature, how only bits and pieces of what happened are left in memory, and the constructive and malleable nature of eyewitness recollections. The three stages of eyewitness information processing are commonly used as an organizational template for presenting this narrative.]

Substantive Questions on Eyewitness Factors

The taxonomy presented below can be used as a menu from which questions can be selected depending on the facts of the case at hand. The number of questions should be limited and the expert's answers should be to the point. Given the often lengthy nature of trial testimony and routine delays, some jurors' attention spans may be taxed and they probably will not be interested in an extended lecture from the expert.

In discussing any one factor, the expert should acknowledge that not all studies follow the majority of outcomes. This practice will avoid the specter of "secrecy" or the appearance of a lack of knowledge on the part of the expert during cross-examination by having the opposing counsel raise these anomalous studies. Also, ethical guidelines established by the American Psychological Association (1981, 1991) admonish experts to discuss the limitations of research that they cite in support of their expert opinion. Adhering to this guideline with respect to such issues as the limitations of laboratory research can head off certain questions that otherwise would be raised on cross-examination and could limit the ultimate impact of the testimony.

M. Are you aware of any studies that have examined the accuracy of eyewitness identifications when the crime was likely to have caused a high level of stress in the witness?

N. Are you aware of any studies that have examined the accuracy of eyewitness identifications when the crime involved a weapon?

O. Are you aware of any studies that have examined the relationship between eyewitnesses' confidence and the accuracy of their identifications?

P. Are you aware of any studies that have examined the accuracy of eyewitness identifications when the assailant and the witness were not of the same race?

Q. Are you aware of any studies that have examined the accuracy of recollections by eyewitnesses from different ethnic backgrounds?

R. Are you aware of any studies that have examined factors that would bias an eyewitness to choose someone from a photoarray or lineup, rather than to state that the suspect is not there?

S. Are you aware of any studies that have examined the effects of an eyewitness receiving new information from someone else prior to viewing a photoarray or lineup?

T. Are you aware of any studies that have examined the effects of an eyewitness seeing a face in the neighborhood prior to their identification of that face in a lineup or in court? [Here reference is made to the phenomenon of unconscious transference.]

U. Are you aware of any studies that have examined the effects of an eyewitness seeing a face in a photo prior to their identification of that face in a lineup or in court? [Here reference is made to carry-over effects.]

V. Are you aware of any studies that have examined the fairness of photoarrays or any related factors that can affect the accuracy of eyewitness identifications?

W. Are you aware of any studies that have examined the accuracy of eyewitness identifications when there was more than one assailant?

X. Are you aware of any studies that have examined the identification accuracy of convenience store clerks?

Y. Are you aware of any studies that have examined the accuracy of police officers as witnesses?

Z. Are you aware of any studies of wrongful convictions caused by faulty eyewitness identifications? [Here reference is made to the surveys of prosecutors and judges concerning faulty convictions, and to the scientific analysis of available cases where convictions were set aside because of new evidence (Goldstein, Chance, & Schneller, 1986; Huff et al., 1986; Rattner, 1988; Wells, 1993). See the discussion of these surveys and analyses in Chapter 2.]

Some judges will sustain objections to question Z as being improper. If such a reaction is anticipated, a more lengthy and explicit version should be used, such as: "Are you aware of any scientifically conducted studies that were designed to determine the most frequent causes of convictions that were later set aside because of new evidence?"

At this point, counsel may elect to pose hypothetical questions to the expert either to summarize the expert's testimony or to link the testimony to the facts in the case. It is especially important that these hypothetical questions be discussed in advance because the eyewitness expert cannot offer an opinion as to whether any given witness is accurate. Also, alternative forms of the hypotheticals should be derived in advance because some judges recently have upheld last-minute motions from opposing counsel to severely curtail the expert in offering an opinion as to the fairness of a particular photoarray or lineup, or even to discuss the explicit elements of the case.

9

Cross-examination Questioning

Cross-examination of technical experts, such as chemists or engineers, usually is a risky business for counsels, but the testimony of the eyewitness expert is more about everyday experience and as such is somewhat more open to scrutiny. This chapter provides guidance for the opposing counsel in preparing the substantive content of a cross-examination of the eyewitness expert. At the same time, this chapter gives the expert advance knowledge of the issues that are likely to be raised. This knowledge may reduce the expert's level of anxiety and ensure more effective testimony. In this regard, the expert should not be surprised should the judge chime in on cross-examination, even with the jury present.

This chapter will deal mainly with the negative thrust of cross-examination questioning and the possible attack on the eyewitness expert and eyewitness psychology. Opposing counsel should bear in mind, however, that most eyewitness situations have their pluses and minuses for each side. Three or four of the factors presented in Chapter 7 might weigh heavily toward the possibility of a mistaken identification, whereas two or three might weight toward an accurate identification. In addition, some factors will carry more weight than others. The weighted ratio of pluses to minuses must be considered by the retaining attorney in making the decision to call the eyewitness expert to the stand in the first place. Opposing counsels should not loose sight of the opportunity to draw out of the expert those factors that are favorable for their side. Thus, the research presented in Chapter 7 should be considered by both sides, and an ethical expert will be forthcoming with appropriate answers based on the vast scientific database from eyewitness psychology. Opposing counsel should expect the expert to qualify his/her answers to address the facts of the case at hand as he/she knows them.

The issues raised by opposing counsel during cross-examination typically overlap with the substantive issues raised by social scientists who are opposed to eyewitness expert testimony. Issues raised by an advocate also are apparent, however. First and foremost, the opposing counsel often will make a direct attack on the credibility of the expert in an attempt to taint the expert testimony before the jury. Melton (1995) reflects that in his experience "the most effective cross-examination, especially of testimony about research findings, is that which obfuscates by deflecting attention away from methodology and central findings to witness credentials..." (p. 90). The expert must be somewhat "thick skinned" and avoid the tendency to take the cross-examination as a personal offense. As an example, I was questioned extensively by one opposing counsel during cross-examination about my compensation for appearing at the trial (he had just completed a successful prosecution in a celebrated case on junk bond dealings). I later was told that in closing arguments, he tended to dwell on my testimony as being a clear case of the "gun for hire" mentality. I am certain that the members of the jury would have been astonished to know that during a recess, this same attorney had chatted with me about his son being a student at UCLA (where I am a professor) and had inquired as to whether I would like to play tennis sometime. It also may be somewhat comforting for the expert to keep in mind that many courtroom observers have noticed the intensity of cross-examination to be directly proportional to the effectiveness of the direct examination.

One of the more difficult forms of cross-examination to entertain is where the opposing counsel, either intentionally or unintentionally, appears not to understand the issues in eyewitness psychology or the purpose of eyewitness expert testimony. This might at first appear to be a case of the opposing counsel "hiding the ball." When the questions do not appear to be logical from either conventional wisdom or expert eyewitness psychology, then the expert must repeatedly ask for clarification and avoid the temptation to read a logical inference into a turgid question. When this happens, the goal of the expert to assist the trier of fact is not likely to be furthered during cross-examination.

A related, intentional tactic that can be used by opposing counsel to "rattle" the expert is to ask several tangential and esoteric questions such as: "You have been throwing out lots of statistics today, so what percentage of eyewitnesses do make accurate identifications?...Well, then, what percentage of eyewitnesses made accurate identifications in the Smith and Jones study you mentioned?" or "What do psychologists mean by validity?" or "What do you mean by Hispanic?" The purpose of these questions is to reduce the expert's confidence during cross-examination and to cast doubt on the knowledge of the expert before the jury. The experienced expert will have already fielded and prepared answers for many of the more esoteric questions. For example, Hispanics can be of any race, but Hispanics in the experiments that I have conducted refers explicitly to Chicano individuals.

For those questions that require more detailed knowledge of specific experiments, the expert should bring key articles and an organized set of supportive materials to the witness stand for reference, especially those that are key to the case at hand. The expert should bring copies of these materials, however, because on rare occasion, the opposing counsel may request that the expert's materials be marked and introduced as exhibits. The Federal Rules of Evidence do not require the disclosure of facts or data underlying an expert opinion offered on direct examination, unless the court requires otherwise. However, "the expert may in any event be required to disclose the underlying facts or data on cross-examination" (Rule 705).

It has been my experience that once opposing counsel detects that I am equipped with a small, organized library, the issue is quickly dropped. I have yet to be met with a request for materials when I inform opposing counsel during cross-examination that I can provide the references upon which I am basing my testimony. I have heard, however, of instances where aggressive attorneys have taken up the expert on such offers. In one case, the expert was asked "Doctor, in this reference you cited as support for your opinion, show me exactly where the sentence is that supports your claim," followed by "So, in fact, doctor, you have been making false representations in your testimony under oath under penalty of perjury, correct?" This "cognitive vivisection" underscores the need for the expert to do the homework in preparation for taking the stand.

Opposing counsel also may try to force the expert into giving an answer to an hypothetical question that has a clear implication but where the answer should be highly qualified. The "common sense" answers may seem obvious to the layperson, and for the expert to give an answer to the contrary would cause the expert to appear irrational. For example, consider the following hypothetical: "Now Dr. Geiselman, wouldn't you be more certain that someone did in fact commit a crime if three people said they saw him do it rather than just one person?" This is a good tactic given that it is well known that jurors are much more impressed by a second witness who makes the same identification than a lone witness who remembers a great deal of detail (Pickel, 1993). Given the facts in the case, however, perhaps the photoarray that was shown to all the witnesses was highly suggestive. Counsel may attempt to prevent the expert from clarifying his/her responses to questions such as these, but the expert and the retaining counsel have at least three options. Above all, the expert should not argue with the opposing counsel.

If the opposing counsel interrupts the expert and does not allow for clarification, the retaining counsel can raise issues of fairness with the judge. This option should be used as a last resort because it may appear to the jury that the expert "needs help" and this may lessen the impact of the testimony. Another option is to go ahead and answer the question with a "yes" or "no" and raise the issue later during re-direct examination for elaboration by the expert. Or, the expert can answer the question with a "yes" or "no" and then immediately ask the judge (never the opposing counsel) for an opportunity to qualify the answer. The request should be made quickly and simply, such as "Your Honor, may I qualify?"

When the cross-examiner consistently cuts off an expert's responses, replete with movements to strike them as nonresponsive, the jurors may become openly frustrated with opposing counsel. In the few cases where I have experienced opposing counsel to persist in the interruption of my answers, several jurors have eventually sighed aloud in apparent frustration. It is known that jurors ponder over what is being kept from them and why (Kalven & Ziesel, 1966; Hastie, Penrod, & Pennington, 1983). The message for the expert is to recognize this probable effect on the jury and avoid becoming defensive, threatened, or argumentative. It also is known that most witnesses who are restricted to yes-or-no answers by the questioner eventually begin to offer only yes-or-no answers (Fisher & Geiselman, 1992). Until the judge instructs the expert to respond otherwise, the expert should avoid compliance with these pressures and continue to respond to opposing counsel's questions as if counsel were not going to interrupt. Should the opposing counsel persist, the message will be sent to the jurors that counsel is attempting to keep something from them that the expert was prepared to offer.

A rare, but annoying tactic used by some opposing counsels is to ask the expert a question, then turn to his/her co-counsel for a mock discussion during the expert's answer. This is an intentional tactic designed to give the impression that the expert's answers are dogmatic and do not really matter. When this has been tried with me, I stop my answer. On one occasion, the opposing counsel stopped with me and said "Go ahead. I can do two things at once." To which I replied "That's Okay, we can wait until you are finished."

In my experience, cross-examination of eyewitness experts usually requires no more than 30 to 40 minutes, but I was cross-examined for over 4 hours on one occasion and I know of one case in Los Angeles where cross-examination of another expert lasted three days. If the opposing counsel chose to delve into the methodologies of the individual studies, or to query the expert extensively about the issues discussed in Chapter 6, then cross-examination would require a good deal of time. The following are some commonly used substantive areas for cross-examination of eyewitness experts. Many of the issues raised here also could be used during an in limine hearing outside the presence of a jury to exclude the eyewitness expert testimony altogether (*People v. Brandon*, 1995). Whether successful or not, an in limine hearing would allow the opponent of expert testimony to assess the expert's responses in advance.

(1) The expert's credibility. A quick look at the expert's resume may be useful to opposing counsel on cross-examination. Depending on the expert, the opposing counsel might ask whether he/she has actually conducted any studies on eyewitness perception and memory. Some persons who have qualified as experts have only read articles and books written by others, and have never actually conducted any of the research themselves.

The opposing counsel might also raise issues about the adversarial flavor of the expert's testimony, including questions that indirectly attack the expert's motivation and objectivity. This can be done in several ways. First, counsel might ask "Who invited you to be here today?" or "Who is paying you to be here." The answer to the second question is somewhat less damaging to an expert who serves on a court panel because the government, not the prosecution or defense, compensates the expert. Opposing counsel might further ask the expert "How much are you being paid for your testimony here today? It's more than $5 per day, isn't it?" One answer that experts can offer is that they are being paid nothing for their testimony, that their testimony cannot be bought, and that they are being compensated for the time that they spent reviewing the documents and giving their opinion in court. The payment issue also can be countered by some experts with a calculation of their fees relative to the estimated number of hours spent in their studies of eyewitness performance. This becomes quite a low figure; in my case at present, the rate is one quarter of one cent per hour. In one case where this issue was overemphasized by opposing counsel, the retaining counsel made the point in closing arguments that everyone in the courtroom is being paid except the audience and the defendant. He forgot that the victim and witnesses were not paid either, but the point was made.

One opposing counsel noticed on my discoverable resume that my first publications in the eyewitness area appeared in 1984. At trial, he asked me if it were just a coincidence that the *McDonald* decision occurred at about the same time as my entering this area or had I viewed *McDonald* as an opening for a lucrative venture. Fortunately, this tactic did not pass muster because I did not testify in court until asked to do so in 1992. This example illustrates, however, that the expert has to be ready for trickery and not passively assume that everyone in the courtroom will appreciate his/her wealth of knowledge.

Opposing counsels almost always explore the expert's history of loyalty by asking "How many times have you testified for the defense and how many times have you testified for the prosecution?" The expert should attempt to qualify the answer by pointing out that one side or the other has never asked him/her to testify, or has only asked him/her to testify "X" times, or has only requested consultations without testimony.

Some counsels also ask experts condescending questions about their degrees such as: "You are not a medical doctor are you?" and "Would you tell us what Ph.D. stands for?" Apparently, it is believed that Doctor of Philosophy does not have the same air of authority to some persons as an M.D. degree. This tactic is used as a smokescreen by some opposing counsels to cast doubt on the authority of the expert's credentials.

Given that there exists a minority view in eyewitness psychology that has been espoused by scientists who would qualify to serve as eyewitness experts, some opposing counsels will ask the testifying expert if he/she has heard of a particular member of this group or researchers. This is followed by a question about whether the expert considers the other scientist to be a reputable member of the scientific community, which is followed in turn by a quote from the scientist such as: "We do not know very much about the factors contributing to eyewitness accuracy" (Elliott, 1993, p. 432). I handle this challenge by simply acknowledging my awareness of the other scientist and my respect for his/her opinions, but that as in any field of science there are differences of opinion and I do not happen to share his/her opinions. Should this line of questioning continue, complete with quote after quote, the retaining attorney should query the expert on re-direct questioning about the surveys of eligible experts which show considerable agreement among those working within eyewitness psychology (Kassin et al., 1989; Kassin & Barndollar, 1992; Yarmey & Jones, 1983).

Probably the ultimate cross-examination "trick" question pertaining to an expert's credibility is: "Has there been any scientific study on the accuracy of your professional judgment?" The implication, of course, is that the expert is an advocate and should have some track record as to innocent versus guilty clients. The expert must re-explain that his/her role is to provide information to the jury about factors that are generally believed to reliably affect the performance of a significant percentage of eyewitnesses, and that he/she is not there to make a judgment about the guilt or innocence of any defendant or even the accuracy of an identification made by any eyewitness.

Aside from these kinds of "fair game" attacks, the expert must understand that some advocates in the system, in my opinion, are not above also engaging in activities that are highly questionable. Those instances of potential misconduct, of course, I must refrain from discussing here.

(2) To establish the "whole" truth. The opposing counsel may choose to raise the issue of selectivity on the part of the expert. The expert is selective in deciding which eyewitness factors to discuss during direct examination and which research studies to cite in support of arguments presented during direct examination. Further, as noted by Melton (1995), "an expert—or any other witness—who seeks to provide the 'whole truth' is likely to have his or her answer stricken from the record as unresponsive to the question posed!" Still further, the extent of selectivity is not totally under the control of the expert because the expert ultimately is not in control of the questions asked during direct examination. One tact for opposing counsel, then, would be to ask the expert for a listing of all the factors that he/she considers when examining a case prior to trial (see

Chapter 7). Opposing counsel may then ask for an opinion concerning each factor as it relates to the present case. In some instances, the jury may get the impression that there are more positive factors than negative factors relevant to the eyewitness evidence. A related tactic would be to question the expert about studies where the outcome runs counter to the argument presented by the expert. With regard to stress, for example, the opposing counsel may question the expert about the Yuille and Cutshall (1986) field study where witnesses' self reports of stress were positively correlated with more accurate reports (see Chapter 7). Chapters 5, 6, and 7 should help the opposing counsel in formulating these strategies, but in some cases, the counsel may choose to employ another expert to aid in the preparation of the case.

(3) Corroborating evidence. Given the facts in the case, opposing counsel could ask the expert about the impact of corroborating evidence on his/her assessment of the reliability of the eyewitness evidence. In many cases, the eyewitness evidence alone may be weak, but other evidence suggests that the defendant is probably guilty of the crime. The expert might respond that it is not his/her expertise to piece together the evidence or to evaluate other forms of evidence. However, the opposing counsel could then counter that this process is exactly how eyewitness evidence is scored for accuracy in field studies on eyewitness performance conducted by social scientists. It is partially because of this issue that counsels should refrain from asking an eyewitness expert to present testimony in cases where the incriminating evidence is substantial against the defendant beyond the eyewitness evidence.

A related tactic that can be used by opposing counsel is to ask the expert how many eyewitnesses it would take for the expert to believe that a suspect is the person who committed a crime. I have seen this question raised both hypothetically and in cases where there were as many as eight eyewitnesses who each selected the defendant independently. In the case of a six-alternative photoarray, the unbiased probability of three witnesses choosing the same person by chance would be one-sixth times one-sixth times one-sixth, or 0.077. Thus, it is unlikely that these witnesses chose the same person by chance. The opposing counsel in one case offered me a calculator so that I could calculate the probability that all the eyewitnesses chose the defendant by chance.

In the case of multiple, concurring witnesses, however, the expert may conclude that there is some problem with either the manner in which the lineup or photoarray was administered or with the composition of the array. Such biasing factors dramatically change the interpretation of the low probability figure. Also, the assumption must be acknowledged that the witnesses who testified in the case were the only ones who were shown the array. Hypothetically, if an investigator were to show an array to enough people, some would identify any given alternative by making a relative judgment. Therefore, when asked questions about the identifications by multiple witnesses, the expert might decline to answer as to how many witnesses it would take or what is the probability of all these witnesses selecting the defendant by chance. Instead, the expert could respond with "I cannot answer that question because to do so would mislead the court." If the opposing counsel does not allow for elaboration, the counsel who called the expert must then raise this issue on re-direct for clarification, especially when it has been documented that other witnesses chose someone else or failed to make an identification.

(4) Relevance to "this" witness. The opposing counsel almost always raises the question of what do these studies tell us about the witness(es) in the case at hand. This question can be stated in several ways such as: "You aren't here to tell us whether Ms. Rodriguez is accurate in her recollections are you?" or "You haven't even talked to Ms. Rodriguez have you?" or "The studies that you have talked about were done with college kids, not like Ms. Rodriguez who is around this sort of thing all the time." In one case, the opposing counsel asked me to calculate what percentage of the studies that I referenced were done on Vietnamese witnesses identifying Nigerians.

This issue draws upon two elements of the debate between social scientists that were presented in Chapter 6, namely the generalizability of the research to the real world and the probabilistic nature of research findings. With respect to the relevancy element, the expert might offer that: "I was not asked to interview Ms. Rodriguez, but I read her statements in the police and investigator reports as well as her testimony at the preliminary hearing. I do not interview the witnesses as an expert on a case because there are no personal characteristics or tests that have been found to reliably predict who will make an accurate eyewitness" (see factor 13 in Chapter 7). With respect to the probabilistic element, the expert must explain that he/she is prepared to discuss factors that are generally believed to reliably affect the performance of a significant percentage of eyewitnesses, but not the performance of any one particular witness. It is up to the jury to apply the expert testimony about the eyewitness factors to the case at hand. If the opposing counsel does not allow for this elaboration, then the counsel who called the expert must raise this issue on re-direct for clarification.

(5) Relevance to the real world. The opposing counsel might call into question the relevance of the studies discussed by the expert to any eyewitness situation. This can be done in several ways such as: "Isn't it true that the people who participate in your experiments know that they are not really witnessing a real crime?" or "Isn't it true that the events that you stage in your experiments are not like real crimes?" In an attempt to illustrate this point to the jury, the opposing counsel in the first case where I appeared approached me on the witness stand and abruptly pointed his finger at my forehead. He shouted "Give me your money!" He was attempting to show that a real victim of such a crime would look at the assailant's face to see what he wanted, rather than at the gun.

In another case, the opposing counsel attempted to refute the "pressure to choose" issue (see Chapter 7) by asking whether I was aware of the hassles that a real witness must endure by coming forward to the authorities, and that students in psychology experiments do not have such pressures. Of course, these counter pressures must be weighed against a witness's initial desire to help, followed by commitment effects. Foster et al. (1994), for example, found that "witnesses" who were led to believe that their identification performance would have direct consequences in a criminal proceeding were no less likely to make a selection than participants who were led to believe that the event was staged as part of an experiment.

Opposing counsel also can refer to the field studies that have produced results counter to the typical outcome of laboratory studies. These include the high level of eyewitness accuracy observed in some field studies (Fisher et al., 1989), the lack of a negative effect of stress on performance (Christianson & Hubinette, 1993; Yuille & Cutshall, 1986), and the apparent lack of weapon focus effects with victims being more accurate than observers (Christianson & Hubinette, 1993).

The expert can offer a discussion of those laboratory experiments that have maintained the ruse of realism from the time of the event through the investigative interview and identification procedure, as well as a discussion of the available field studies of actual cases (see Chapter 6 on this issue). Again, if the expert is not allowed to elaborate on cross, then the counsel who requested the expert must raise this issue on re-direct examination.

(6) Scrutiny of specific experiments. Some counsels may choose to question the expert during cross-examination about the methodology, results, and interpretation of specific experiments cited by the expert during direct examination. The results of any particular experiment are open to some interpretation. Egeth (1993), for example, summarized the experiments on carry-over effects and concluded that "it does not seem possible to base any useful testimony to a jury on these experimental reports." There may have been some unforeseen, extraneous influence on the outcome of any experiment. Perhaps the control group was not appropriate. Perhaps the effect of a factor on eyewitness performance is statistically reliable, but it is nonetheless relatively small. The size of the cross-racial identifica-

tion effect, for example, typically is only a 10-to-15 percent difference in performance (see Chapter 7).

Given that expert testimony is exempt from the Hearsay rule (Federal Rules of Evidence 703) and opposing counsels cannot cross-examine other researchers cited by the expert, they must become conversant with the basic literature presented and critiqued in Chapters 5, 6, and 7. Unless opposing counsels have the opportunity to take a course on research methodology and eyewitness performance at a college or university, they may want to call an expert of their own to aid them in a critical evaluation of specific experiments. Workshops by reputable experts for either Public Defender's or District Attorney's Offices may be an efficient alternative if enough time can be taken away from actual cases by a group.

(7) Attacking the social science. Some opposing counsels choose to engage in an attack on the discipline of social science from which the research is drawn. The bulk of the attack typically takes place during closing arguments with references to the "ivory tower" and statements such as: "It's sort of insulting" and "You don't need them to tell you how to think." An opposing counsel in a recent celebrated case explained to the jury during closing arguments that she did not call an expert for her side because she "did not want to glorify them." She later told me that expert opinion in the field that was relevant to the matter simply did not support the side that she was empowered to advocate.

On occasion, opposing counsel also will attempt to chip away at the social science during cross-examination of the expert. In one case, mentioned earlier, the opposing counsel asked me about the use of rats in experiments on stress. I fortunately was allowed to describe the vast literature that is based on experiments with humans, including experiments dealing directly with eyewitness situations. Nevertheless, some jurors may have been affected by the implication that the expert comes from a field where some researchers still study rats. Another opposing counsel denounced psychology as an inexact discipline and literally shouted "You can't tell what's going on up here, can you (pointing at his head)!" Whether it was a good idea or not, I replied "That's correct counsel, and let's hope that you are not basing your whole case on what you think is going on up there." Such argumentative responses by the expert typically are not advised, however.

Another tactic is to portray psychology as "wizardry" or as a "soft" science. On several occasions, I have been asked questions on cross-examination such as: "Psychology is not like chemistry or physics is it? I mean, it's not even been around for very long, has it?" There are several responses to this attack. First, social scientists utilize the same experimental methods that are used by chemists and physicists. They establish control groups and they conduct experiments in which factors of interest are manipulated to determine the effects of those factors on performance. See Chapter 5 for a more elaborate exposition of the experimental methodology used in eyewitness psychology. Second, the first recognized psychological laboratory was established by Wundt in 1879, with the first recognized book on cognitive psychology being published by William James in 1890. Third, and more to the point, the first recognized book on eyewitness psychology was published by Munsterberg in 1908. Thus, psychology, cognitive psychology, and eyewitness psychology have been recognized as credible forms of science for quite a while.

10

Preparing for Re-direct Questioning

As with any witness testimony, the quality of eyewitness expert testimony depends heavily on re-direct questioning. An understanding of the issues presented in Chapters 6 and 9 should facilitate the interaction between expert and attorney in formulating a strategy for re-direct questioning in advance of the expert taking the stand. Advance preparation for re-direct questioning also will give counsel a general feeling for whether he/she should pursue certain issues raised by opposing counsel with the expert during cross-examination. The expert cannot signal counsel during cross-examination and there is a rule of thumb that an expert should not even look at the retaining counsel while responding during cross-examination (see Chapter 11). Therefore, the attorney and expert must plan for re-direct questioning in advance, and this process depends mainly on the expert. With all due respect, there is an old adage that trial lawyers dream about cross-examination of witnesses at the expense of planning for the questioning of their own witnesses. Some eyewitness experts may have appeared in more trials that revolve exclusively around eyewitness testimony than the retaining attorney.

It is easy to understand the frustration of being on the witness stand and not being able to suggest questions to counsel following cross-examination. In one case, the opposing counsel asked me to calculate the probability that five eyewitnesses would have all selected the defendant by chance. I could only begin my response with "Assuming that the photoarray was fair and the tests were conducted in a fair manner..." Fortunately, the retaining counsel had the presence of mind to question me further about the limiting conditions of my calculation during re-direct examination.

If needed, the expert's credentials can be revived by asking: "How many years did you spend at the university studying for your degrees?" or "Would a medical degree have helped you in your expert evaluation of the evidence in this case?" or "You are not the only social scientist who studies eyewitness performance, are you?" or "Isn't it true that there is an entire division of the American Psychological Association that is devoted to issues directly relevant to your testimony here today?" or "Isn't it true that there have been thousands of experiments conducted on eyewitness perception and memory?"

If needed, the "gun for hire" issue can be countered by asking any of the following questions: "Serving as an expert is not your primary source of income is it?" "You weren't just waiting around for this case to come along were you?" "Would your testimony have changed if you were not paid for your services?"

The first four issues for cross-examination listed in Chapter 9 can be handled by the expert on re-direct examination simply with requests for clarification from counsel. In contrast, it typically is not possible to prepare for re-direct questioning about any specific experiments attacked by the opposing counsel, or any specific experiments raised in apparent conflict with those discussed by the expert. Whether or not to pursue those arguments and additional studies for clarification is a judgment call and can only be calculated through advance interaction between counsel and the expert. Joint review of Chapters 7 and 8 should enhance this interaction.

Another tactic that a defense counsel might use during re-direct examination is to ask the expert "How should the investigators have done it in this case?" Depending on the facts of the case, the expert might respond that the alternative persons in the lineup should have reflected the witnesses' pre-lineup verbal descriptions. Or, the photoarray should have been tested for fairness with mock witnesses who are asked to guess the suspect from the witnesses' verbal descriptions. Or, there should have been a proper set of instructions given to the witnesses with a more unbiased presentation. Or, the investigators should have shown the witnesses a lineup that did not contain the suspect first. Or, they should have presented the alternatives one at a time rather than all together. With a complete combination of these procedures, Wells (1993) estimates that rates of false identifications can be very low, as little as two percent. When using this tactic, the expert must be sure to explain that these are ideal procedures that have been shown to be effective in controlled experiments, and that things are more difficult to control in the real world. The contrast (or lack thereof) between this ideal set of procedures and the procedures actually used in the case could be informative to the trier of fact.

11

Courtroom Demeanor of the Expert

There are a few treatments of courtroom demeanor for counsels and experts (Bank & Poythress, 1982, The elements of persuasion in expert testimony; O'Barr, 1982, Linguistic evidence: Language, power, and strategy in the courtroom; Cooke, 1990, Survival in the witness box; Herbert & Barrett, 1980, Attorney's master guide to courtroom psychology). These treatments include recommendations on how to speak and phrase questions and responses to questions, where to stand in the courtroom during different portions of the trial, and when to look toward the witness, judge, and jury. According to O'Barr (1982), for example, a powerless speech style in the courtroom is characterized by verbal hedges ("sort of" or "maybe"), intensifiers ("very" or "definitely"), hesitations ("uh" or "you know"), and a high incidence of gesturing. In contrast, powerful speech contains few instances of these characteristics. Mock jurors who observe powerless testimony judge the witness (expert or otherwise) to be less convincing and truthful, as well as less competent and intelligent (Lisko, 1993). I will defer the reader to those sources for further such suggestions for counsels and experts. The present chapter focuses on a selected set of recommendations concerning courtroom demeanor specifically for the eyewitness expert based on my observations and experiences in and around the courtroom. Additional guidelines specifically for psychologists serving as experts, including standard courtroom procedure and etiquette, can be found in Blau's (1984) The psychologist as expert witness and in Carson's (1990) Professionals and the courts: a handbook for expert witnesses.

Before discussing demeanor in the courtroom, the expert and attorney must consider demeanor in the hallway. I try to wait some distance away from the jury until they enter the courtroom. Aside from being counter to judge's instructions, any direct or indirect interaction could alter a juror's thinking or the expert's thinking. Consider the following incident that happened to me. The retaining attorney had told me to go to Department "E," so I sat next to Department "F" because both juries were assembled in the hallway. I overheard two jurors from Department "F" talking about how the use of experts in the Menendez trial was a rape of the taxpayers' money. Boy, was I glad that they were not on my jury! I would have been made somewhat nervous having heard those remarks. Unfortunately, the retaining attorney had told me to appear at the wrong department. These individuals were from my jury, and now I was conscious of the impending attack on my fee structure by the opposing counsel. I had enough experience at that point to refrain from being overly defensive about my fees on cross-examination, but if this incident had occurred much earlier in my experience as an expert, perhaps things would have been different. It is best not to hear what jurors say in the hallway. It is likewise best that the jurors not see you in what could be interpreted as a scheming conversation with the retaining attorney. Decide upon the content and format of the direct-examination testimony before arriving at court.

Message Style

The eyewitness expert must keep the testimony focused on the general psychological phenomena rather than on the particular eyewitnesses in a case. As mentioned at several points in this book, eyewitness psychology is a probabilistic science. The eyewitness expert can present to the jury the factors that are generally believed to reliably affect the performance of a significant percentage of eyewitnesses. Once the expert is drawn into a discussion about the particular witnesses in a case, the testimony can quickly degenerate to a level of mere speculation. When this happens, the jury will become offended by the presence of the expert. Because the expert is not likely to have interviewed the witnesses, the jury may feel that they "know" the witnesses better than the expert at this point.

The eyewitness expert should use lay language and avoid using technical jargon such as "blank lineups" or "cue utilization." These terms may impress colleagues at a convention, but it probably does little to impress the members of a jury. In this regard, the most qualified expert is not necessarily the best witness. The witness must be able to communicate with the jurors as laypersons without being condescending. A results of a major survey of jurors and judges indicated that the single most important element of effective expert testimony is the ability to convey technical information in non-technical language (Shuman, Whitaker, & Champagne, 1994). Even relatively simple concepts should be defined in terms of their function, such as the purpose of a "control group" in an experiment. This practice conveys to the jury that the expert is there to assist them as the triers of fact and not to impress them with "book knowledge." Before testifying, the expert should ask the attorney about the demographics of the jurors and their responses during voir dire, as well as the judge's background, style, and expectancies. This information will help the expert to refine his/her message style to be more acceptable to the trier of fact. Expressing eyewitness psychology in simple terms and in an acceptable manner does not require experts to overgeneralize or to underqualify their testimony, however (Elliott, 1993).

When discussing a particular eyewitness factor, the expert should acknowledge at the outset that "lay" assumptions about eyewitness performance are logical. Otherwise, the common sense of the jurors will contradict the expert's testimony. For example, when presenting the scientific evidence on weapon focus, the expert should state that it makes sense that "I'll never forget his face because he pointed the gun at me," but that the evidence does not necessarily support this belief and here is why. When presenting the scientific evidence on confidence, the expert should state that it makes sense that someone who is confident should be more accurate than someone who is unsure, but that the evidence does not necessarily support this belief and here is why. When presenting the scientific evidence on unconscious transference, the expert should state that it makes sense that having seen someone before should help a witness's performance, but that the evidence does not necessarily support this belief and here is why. In this manner, the expert is acknowledging that before his/her experience as a researcher in eyewitness psychology, he/she may also have believed in these common-sense assumptions.

Whom to Address

On direct examination, the expert should address his/her remarks to the jury. This serves to develop rapport and to promote the more credible "educator" role of the expert (Beebe, 1974) as opposed to an advocate role. The remarks should include embellishments and examples to clarify the concepts that are being presented. In contrast, on cross-examination, the expert sometimes should address some of his/her responses to the judge. This is especially the case when the opposing counsel inappropriately attacks the expert. Answering only to the opposing counsel under such conditions gives credence to the counsel's adversarial questions, and addressing the jury could appear as seeking approval for the answers being given. Addressing the answers to the judge serves to acknowledge that the court demands the expert to comply with the cross-examination questions while not necessarily giving the questions any credence. Requests to be allowed to clarify an answer or to briefly examine reference materials also should be addressed to the judge and never the opposing counsel. When clarification is not warranted, the expert should answer cross-examination questions to the point, without volunteering additional information. During lengthy delays or side-bar conferences, the expert may want to glance to the jury periodically to re-affirm that he/she is there to assist them in their task and to maintain an ongoing level of rapport.

Body Positioning and Voice

It is commonly suggested that any witness should sit up straight with their arms on the table and their fingers loosely clasped. This body positioning confirms to the jury that the witness is calm, yet is taking the act of offering the testimony quite seriously. The expert's answers to questions from opposing counsel during cross-examination must be direct and presented in a quiet, unthreatened manner. A more comprehensive and witty treatment of issues such as these is provided by psychologist Stanley Brodsky (1991) for clinicians testifying as expert witnesses. He suggests that experts vary the loudness of their voices, speak slowly, stress certain syllables to maintain the jurors' attention, and ease into their breath patterns to promote the appearance of calmness.

12

Ethical Dilemmas for Psychologists as Experts

Consultant-Advocate Distinction

The eyewitness expert typically serves as a consultant on behalf of either the defense or the prosecution in the adversarial system. One of the more difficult tasks of the expert is to remain in the role of consultant (albeit an advocate for the expert's own testimony) and not stray into the role of an advocate for the retaining side. This dilemma for the expert has been addressed in a special issue of *Ethics and Behavior* (Sales & Shuman, 1993). See also Bersoff's (1995) Contemporary conflicts in ethics for psychology. The *Specialty Guidelines for Forensic Psychologists* (American Psychological Association, 1991) state that: "The forensic psychologist [should] take special care to avoid undue influence upon their methods, procedures, and products, such as might emanate from the party to a legal proceeding by financial compensation or other gains." The expert who serves on a court panel has a somewhat easier task than an expert who is not suggested to counsel by the court. Specifically, an expert's reputation among attorneys as being willing to selectively provide "what is needed" to strengthen a case is not as likely to be a significant temptation for the court panel expert. This is not to imply that most experts will be tempted or that attorneys even prefer an advocate to an expert who is fair, impartial, and an educator. Nonetheless, the goals of the adversarial system are different from the goals of the scientific community.

Consider, for example, the views of one distinguished lawyer: "Many people are convinced that the expert who really persuades a jury is the independent, objective, nonarticulate type... I disagree. I would go into a lawsuit with an objective, uncommitted, independent expert about as willingly as I would occupy a fox-hole with a couple of non-combatant soldiers" (Meier, 1982). This perception is shared by some psychologists. Elliott (1993) writes that "lawyers and other policy actors will almost always choose advocates over impartial scientists, which only means that the adversary system is not a fit environment for science" (p. 435). In contrast, the *Specialty Guidelines for Forensic Psychologists* (American Psychological Association, 1991) state that forensic psychologists must not "engage in partisan distortion or misrepresentation. Forensic psychologists do not, by either commission or omission, participate in a misrepresentation of their evidence, nor do they participate in partisan attempts to avoid, deny, or subvert the presentation of evidence contrary to their own position." Aside from the ethical obligation to be objective, a survey of judges revealed that, while most felt many expert witnesses appeared to give the impression of bias in their testimony, "judges and juries are more impressed by an impartial, objective, scientific presentation" (Corder, Spalding, Whiteside, & Whiteside, 1990).

Regardless of how an attorney acquires an eyewitness expert, either by reputation or by appearing on a court panel of experts, the fact is that most often the client appearing on the paperwork is the defendant. In some cases, this arrangement has led to in-person consultation with the defendant. With *Propria-Persona* cases, this interaction is almost a certainty. In other cases, attorneys may even introduce the expert to the defendant's family in the hallways of the courthouse. Across trials, additional pressures to become adversarial may mount on the expert, with repeated attacks from opposing counsels during cross-examination and the rare, off-color comments from opposing parties outside the courtroom (Loftus & Ketcham, 1991). The sum of these pressures has led some to question the ability of individual scientists to present accurate and unbiased summaries of the scientific literature (Saks, 1990).

In the face of significant social pressures that are created by these interactions, the expert must remain objective in his/her evaluation of the eyewitness evidence and be willing to present the "whole" truth in any written report and at trial. This practice is mandated in Principle 4(g) of the *Ethical Principles of Psychologists* (APA, 1981, p. 635). There is no substitute for a frank exchange at the outset between counsel and expert about the consultant role, and what this implies for the impending evaluation of the eyewitness evidence. Anything less will catch up with the expert in due time (Loftus, 1986), while leaving the counsel looking a bit clever for the moment but without the expert for the future. What future lawyers will look for is the expert's reputation.

Contact from "The Other Side"

Related to the dilemma of advocating the retaining attorney's position is the dilemma created when the counsel for the opposing party makes contact with the expert. There would be no conflict created by the expert discussing his or her credentials with the opposing counsel. There also would be no harm in discussing the factors that are typically presented in eyewitness expert testimony. Indeed, these factors are laid out in this book as well as in other sources. Ethical and legal problems may arise, however, should the expert discuss specific elements of the case with the opposing counsel or discuss any information about the case supplied in confidence by the retaining attorney. This is especially true if the expert is not presently included on the witness list, and this holds regardless of whether the expert is appointed by the court or retained by a private attorney. There also is considerable legal and ethical controversy on this issue. Therefore, when contacted by an opposing counsel, I respectfully explain that I would be happy to discuss the case when either (1) I am advised in writing by the retaining counsel that I am free to converse about the facts of the case, including the anticipated contents of my testimony about the facts of the case, or (2) I am ordered in writing by the court to converse about the facts of the case, including the anticipated contents of my testimony concerning the facts of the case. I leave the resolution of both of these tasks to the opposing counsel who has made contact with me.

Protecting the Innocent Versus Freeing the Guilty

The Ethics Code of the American Bar Association admonishes defense counsels to defend their clients zealously. Prosecution counsel's adversarial role is to see that justice is done. The eyewitness expert's consultant role is to objectively evaluate the eyewitness evidence provided and perhaps to request additional information relevant to the evaluation. Some experts believe that willingness to testify on behalf of a client should be partially dependent on whether he/she believes in the defendant's guilt or innocence. Others believe that this is a dangerous practice because the expert could be incorrect in the assessment of guilt. Furthermore, it has been my experience that the totality of evidence can change dramatically between the time the expert is first consulted and the time of trial. Still others believe that guilt or innocence is totally irrelevant to the eyewitness expert's evaluation of the eyewitness portion of the evidence. Ensuring appropriate police and prosecutorial procedures in the future may be enough justification for some experts to testify in some cases.

Regardless of the expert's position, it is almost always the case that the file presented to the expert contains information other than eyewitness evidence, and it sometimes implies that the defendant is guilty. Either the defendant already has an extensive criminal record for the offense with which he is now charged, or there may even be physical evidence such as a fingerprint. However, even accepting the otherwise reliable fingerprint as damning evidence may give some experts pause in light of the recent cases from other jurisdictions such as New York State where fingerprint evidence was falsified.

In cases where the only evidence is the eyewitness evidence, the ethical dilemma is still present for the expert in both directions. This is especially pronounced with capital crimes. Consider the following case in which I was appointed by the Superior Court of Los Angeles as the eyewitness expert. An armored car courier was transporting a bag of money down an isle of a large department store when he was shot from behind by a lone assailant. The assailant proceeded to place his handgun to the temple of the victim and fire additional rounds to ensure the victim's death. The assailant then fled. There was a single eyewitness who saw the assailant run directly passed him with gun drawn before ducking behind a door. The witness worked with a police sketch artist to form a composite that was given to the news media. A woman who saw the composite in a newspaper phoned the police and stated that this man had shot her son several years earlier in a drug-related incident. The authorities then arrested the man who had been convicted of her son's shooting (the suspect was now on parole), and placed his photo in a 6-pack array. This array was shown to the lone eyewitness who selected the suspect's photo with great confidence. As I understood the matter, the eyewitness stood to gain considerable reward money and the defendant stood to loose his life.

On the one hand, most observers would probably say that the person responsible for this heinous act deserves the death penalty. It gave me great pause to consider that I might play an integral part in freeing a man who committed such a crime. He had in fact already shot another person in a prior case. On the other hand, the reader only has to skim through Chapter 7 to find grist enough for extensive eyewitness expert testimony in this case. Stress, weapon focus, confidence, carry-over effects, and pressures to choose all were issues. And what if the defendant were innocent of this crime? Should a reluctant expert pass this case along to another expert, who is perhaps less qualified but willing to "do the job?" There are no fixed solutions to this dilemma, but it is a choice that each expert eventually must face.

Accepting and Declining Cases

It is important for both counsel and expert to accept that there will be some cases where the expert must decline a case because it hits too close to home and might jeopardize his/her ability to effectively carry out the consultant role. A survey of potential eyewitness experts showed that more respondents said they had refused to testify at least once than respondents who said they had testified at least once (Kassin et al., 1989). Loftus refers to one case in which she declined to testify on behalf of a suspected Nazi war criminal (Loftus & Ketcham, 1991). I also declined a case where a young Asian gang member was accused of holding a knife to a three-month-old baby's throat while demanding the mother's wedding ring. The accused had no prior arrest record, maintained his innocence, and the only evidence against him was the husband's photoarray identification. The mother stated that she did not recognize the defendant. Nevertheless, I had a four-month-old baby at the time and could not suppress my empathy for the victim. My reasons for declining this case were as much to do with my concern about the defendant's potential innocence as with my disgust for the act. In this case, I decided that the court's interests would be better served by an expert who would not have the strong personal associations to the facts of the case. Other experts might, of course, have the same kinds of associations to the facts in other cases and would choose to defer those cases to other experts.

There is no substitute for frank discussions of these issues at the outset between counsel and expert. Such discussion often can avert misunderstandings about the concerns and agendas of counsel as well. A few defense attorneys have requested that I review eyewitness evidence for their clients so that they could convince their clients that there were no arguable issues concerning the eyewitness evidence in their cases, and therefore they should agree to plea-bargains.

13

Alternatives to Eyewitness Expert Testimony

Judge's Model Instructions to the Jury

Results from mock-trial studies suggest that voir dire is not an adequate safeguard for identifying and excusing prospective jurors who are unable or unwilling to critically evaluate eyewitness testimony (Narby & Cutler, 1994). A second safeguard is the reading of judge's cautionary instructions on eyewitness identification at the conclusion of the trial. This is the preferred alternative to eyewitness expert testimony in the United Kingdom (Lord Devlin, 1976, the Turnbull judgments). Over the past 20 years, both federal and state courts in the United States also have encouraged judges to read instructions to jurors that specify factors they should consider when evaluating eyewitness evidence. In *Neil v. Biggers* (1972), the U.S. Supreme Court listed five factors that should be contained in judge's instructions to the jury in cases where eyewitness evidence is central to the case. These factors are: The opportunity for witnesses to view the criminal at the time of the crime, the length of time between the crime and the later identification, the level of certainty shown by the witnesses at the identification, the witnesses' degree of attention during the crime, and the accuracy of the witnesses' prior description of the criminal.

More recently, in *State v. Warren* (1981), Kansas judges were encouraged to instruct jurors in the following seven factors: The opportunity the witness had to observe, the emotional state of the witness including that which might be caused by the use of a weapon, whether the witness had observed the defendant(s) on earlier occasions, whether a significant amount of time elapsed between the crime and later identification, whether the witness ever failed to identify the defendant(s) or made any inconsistent identification, the degree of certainty demonstrated by the witness, and whether there are any other circumstances that may have affected the accuracy of the eyewitness identification.

A major difference between eyewitness expert testimony and these model instructions from a judge is that the factors are listed without any clear guidance to the jurors on how to interpret those factors. For example, both sets of instructions include a reference to the eyewitnesses' level of certainty, but most jurors would probably infer that this means a confident witness should be believed and a witness who is uncertain should be less believed. The majority of laboratory and field evidence suggests that this is not the case (see factor 3). Further, in Biggers a reference is made to the accuracy of the witnesses' prior description, but the available evidence shows that we cannot predict the accuracy of an identification from a witnesses' prior verbal description (Deffenbacher, 1991; Pigott & Brigham, 1985; Wells, 1985). Thus, the lack of specificity of the model instructions suggests that they would not be an effective alternative to eyewitness expert testimony.

There has been some research carried out on the effectiveness of another set of model instructions that arose from *U.S. v.*

Telfaire (1972). In that case, Melvin Telfaire was found guilty of robbery based on the sole identification of a Mr. Peregory. No other persons witnessed the robbery and no physical evidence was ever recovered. The court of appeals overturned the conviction on the premise that the trial court had failed "to give a special instruction on identification in which the case turned on the testimony of a single witness," even in the absence of a request by the defense counsel. The appeals court concluded that "trial courts should as a matter of routine include an identification instruction which emphasizes to the jury the need for finding that the circumstances of identification are convincing, ...and in cases where identification is a major issue, the court should not rely on defense counsel to request such a charge." The *Telfaire* instructions make some reference to half of the factors listed in Chapter 7, such as the confidence and carry-over effect issues, but these instructions show the same lack of specificity as the Biggers and Warren instructions. It is not surprising, therefore, that the *Telfaire* instructions have not been found to sensitize jurors to the eyewitnessing and identification conditions in a case (Cutler et al., 1990; Greene, 1988). In fact, there is some evidence that these instructions can dramatically bias jurors' verdicts one way or the other depending on when during a trial the judge chooses to read the instructions (Ramirez et al., 1996).

Amicus Curiae Briefs

Another alternative to eyewitness expert testimony is for social scientists to submit amicus curiae or "friend of the court" briefs to the courts (Roesch, Golding, Hans, & Reppucci,

1991). Amicus briefs summarize available research that is considered relevant to a particular case and presents implications of the research for the issues in the case. This activist role for social scientists has been supported by some (Tremper, 1987) and criticized by others (Elliott, 1993; Konecni & Ebbesen, 1986). On the positive side, these briefs may be prepared by several authors who include a list of references to document their conclusions, and the brief may be reviewed by others, including APA boards and committees, prior to submission to the court. Finally, the authors and supporters typically are not paid for their services in preparing or reviewing the brief. On the surface, then, amicus curiae briefs might appear to be more credible to the courts.

On the other hand, it would be hard to overlook the possibility that some scientists writing briefs would have biased views just as would some experts who appear in court. Some would have hidden agendas and future advantages to the authors could drive some briefs. Konecni and Ebbesen (1986) caution that amicus briefs "would be paraded as neutral, objective, scientifically unimpeachable information," but would reflect "entrenched views by a few recognized authorities" (p. 123). Some respected scientists would sign briefs in support of the underlying premise without even reading the brief because of time constraints. The potential for a "battle of the briefs" via facsimile machines would be at least as likely as a "battle of the experts" in court. Others also have questioned whether judges and juries can adequately interpret and criticize the briefs on their own without an adversarial cross-examination (Elliott, 1993). Most of the criticisms of eyewitness expert testimony presented in Chapter 6 apply to amicus briefs as well because they concern the body of research upon which the briefs would be based. Finally, this option would appear to have limited application at present for addressing eyewitness issues in legal cases, except in "trouble cases" at the appellate court level (Diamond, 1989), because trial courts have historically made little use of briefs in lieu of experts.

Benefits and Consequences of Doing Nothing

The view that eyewitness experts should stay out of the courtroom has been around at least since the turn of the century (Wigmore, 1909) and has been considered by more recent scholars (Egeth, 1995; McCloskey & Egeth, 1983; Konecni & Ebbesen, 1986; McKenna et al., 1992). Doing nothing could speed up some trials and would save the government and the people some money if the decisions are not overturned. Given the debate described in Chapter 6, as well as evidence from some mock-trial experiments that eyewitness identifications can be neutralized somewhat through effective cross-examination (Kennedy & Haygood, 1992), it must be questioned whether social scientists should appear in court as eyewitness experts. Strategies for the cross-examination of eyewitnesses can be found in Bailey and Rothblatt (1985) and Bailey and Fishman (1995). Most of the evidence from mock-trial research, however, casts doubt on the effectiveness of cross-examination with confident witnesses, and these are the very witnesses whom jurors place a great deal of weight (Lindsay, Wells, & O'Connor, 1989; Wells, Lindsay, & Ferguson, 1979).

With respect to the reliability of the research base, Yarmey (1986) asserts that "if experimental psychologists never acted until they were absolutely sure of the scientific results they would never leave the laboratory." Konecni and Ebbesen (1986) caution that "no intervention seems clearly preferable to an intervention of dubious value, especially when one is dealing with a highly sensitive area where people's lives (the defendant's, the victim's, the potential future victims') are quite literally at stake." Loftus (1983) responds that "silence is not golden" and "when prominent members of the legal field say that testimony based on psychological research offers a 'beacon of hope,' it makes me feel pretty good about what I'm doing."

Deffenbacher (1984) concludes that "we can and should encourage jurors to reduce the weight put on eyewitness testimony, particularly where it has not received truly independent corroboration by other witnesses or by physical evidence." McCloskey and Egeth (1984) counter with "what is needed is not expert testimony to induce a general increase in juror skepticism, but rather testimony that brings juror evaluations more in line with actual witness performance." There is evidence from mock-trial studies that jurors spend more time deliberating (Maass, Brigham, & West, 1985) and focus more time on the eyewitness evidence (Hosch, Beck, & McIntyre (1980) when an eyewitness expert is allowed to testify. The available research concerning the effect of eyewitness expert testimony on juror sensitivity to the evidence is somewhat mixed. There are some findings that jurors become more sensitized to eyewitnessing and identification conditions with the aid of the expert testimony (Blonstein & Geiselman, 1990; Cutler et al., 1989; Loftus, 1980; Wells & Wright, 1983), while the results of other studies suggest that jurors simply become more skeptical of eyewitnesses in general (Cutler et al., 1990; Lindsay, 1994; Wells, Lindsay, & Tousignant, 1980). Cutler et al. (1989) found that without expert testimony, mock jurors did not make any use of their purported knowledge of eyewitnessing factors, but instead relied heavily upon the confidence expressed by the eyewitnesses. In contrast, testimony from an eyewitness expert served to sensitize the jurors to the witnessing and identification conditions presented in the evidence, and desensitized them to the confidence expressed by the eyewitnesses. Still, Fox and Walters (1986) found expert testimony to have a greater effect on mock jurors' perceptions of eyewitnesses who expressed low confidence than high confidence.

Ultimately, the decision to allow eyewitness experts to testify at trial is with the courts. "It will be the law and not psychology that will decide if, and under what conditions, experts on eyewitness identification will be allowed to testify" (Lempert, 1986, p. 181). Over the recent objections by some (Elliott, 1993; McKenna et al., 1992), eyewitness expert testimony is becoming more and more common and the weight of expert opinion appears to favor this practice (Kassin et al., 1994; Cutler & Penrod, 1995). Melton (1987, p. 488) has reviewed instances where each member of the U.S. Supreme Court has either approved the admission of social-science testimony or criticized other justices for not allowing such testimony. It also is notable that one long-time critic of eyewitness expert testimony has written in 1995: "I think it is important that we *not* (my italics) abandon the effort to understand the effects of all of the factors that affect eyewitness testimony. Such work is complex and very difficult but the potential benefits to society are commensurately great" (Egeth, 1995, p. 163). It is hoped that this book will provide a basis for enhancing the interaction between counsel and the eyewitness expert in the preparation of cases and in the evaluation of eyewitness evidence under current procedures.

References

Ainsworth PB: Incident perception by British police officers. Law & Human Behavior 1981; 5:2-3:231-236

Allport GW, Postman LJ: The psychology of rumor, in Readings in Social Psychology. Edited by Maccoby EE, Newcomb TM, Hartley EL. New York, Holt, Rinehart, and Winston, 1958

Alper A, Buckhout R, Chern S, Harwood R, Slomovits M: Eyewitness identification: accuracy of individual vs. composite recollections of a crime. Bulletin of the Psychonomic Society 1976; 8:147-149

American Psychological Association: Ethical Principles of Psychologists. Washington, DC, American Psychological Association, 1981, 1991

American Psychological Association: Specialty guidelines for forensic psychologists. Law and Human Behavior 1991; 15:655-665

Anderson CA, Lepper MR, Ross L: Perseverance of social theories: the role of explanation in the persistence of discredited information. Journal of Personality and Social Psychology 1980; 39:1037-1049

Anderson, KJ: Arousal and the inverted-U hypothesis: a critique of Neisser's "reconceptualizing arousal." Psychological Bulletin 1990; 107:96-100

Anthony T, Copper C, Mullen B: Cross-racial facial identification: a social cognitive integration. Personality and Social Psychology Bulletin 1992; 18:296-301

Ayuk RE: Cross-racial identification of transformed, untransformed, and mixed-race faces. International Journal of Psychology 1990; 25:509-527

Bailey FL, Fishman KJ: Criminal trial techniques. New York, Clark, Boardman, & Callaghan, 1995

Bailey FL, Rothblatt HB: Successful techniques for criminal trials (2nd Ed). Rochester, New York, Lawyers Co-operative, 1985

Bank S, Poythress N: The elements of persuasion in expert testimony. Journal of Psychiatry and Law 1982; 10:173-204

Barkowitz P, Brigham JC: Recognition of faces: own-race bias, incentive, and time delay. Journal of Applied Social Psychology 1982; 12:255-268

Bartlett JC, Leslie JE: Aging and memory for faces versus single views of faces. Memory and Cognition 1986; 14:371-381

Bazelon DL: Veils, values, and social responsibility. American Psychologist 1982; 37:115-121

Beebe SA: Eye contact: a nonverbal determinant of speaker credibility. The Speech Teacher 1974; 23:21-25

Behrman BW, Vayder LT: The biasing influence of a police showup: does the observation of a single suspect taint later identification? Perceptual & Motor Skills 1994; 79:1239-1248

Bekerian DA, Dennett JL: The cognitive interview technique: reviving the issues. Applied Cognitive Psychology 1993; 7:275-297

Bekerian DA: In search of the typical eyewitness. American Psychologist 1993 48:574-576

Belli RF, Windschitl PD, McCarthy TT, Winfrey SE: Detecting memory impairment with a modified test procedure: manipulating retention interval with centrally presented event items. Journal of Experimental Psychology: Learning, Memory, and Cognition 1992; 18:356-367

Bem DJ: Self-perception theory, in Advances in Experimental Social Psychology, Volume 6. Edited by Berkowitz L. San Diego, Academic Press, 1972; 1-62

Bermant G: Two conjectures about the issue of expert testimony. Law and Human Behavior 1986; 10:97-100

Bersoff DN: Contemporary conflicts in ethics for psychology. Washington, DC, American Psychological Association, 1995

Black B, Singer JA: From Frye to Daubert: a new test for scientific evidence. Shepard's Expert and Scientific Quarterly 1993; 1:16-41

Blau TH: The Psychologist as Expert Witness. New York, John Wiley & Sons, 1984

Blonstein R, Geiselman E: Effects of witnessing conditions and expert witness testimony on credibility of an eyewitness. American Journal of Psychology 1990; 6:11-19

Boon JCW, Davies GM: Attitudinal influences on witness memory: fact and fiction, in Practical Aspects of Memory: Current Research and Issues, Volume I. Edited by Gruneberg MM, Morris PE, Sykes RN. Chichester, Wiley, 1988; 53-58

Bothwell RK, Brigham JC, Malpass RS: Cross-racial identification. Personality and Social Psychology Bulletin 1989; 15:19-25

Bothwell RK, Brigham JC, Pigott, MA: An exploratory study of personality differences in eyewitness memory. Journal of Social Behavior & Personality 1987; 2:335-343

Bothwell RK, Deffenbacher KA, Brigham JC : Correlation of eyewitness accuracy and confidence: optimality hypothesis revisited. Journal of Applied Psychology 1987; 72:691-695

Brigham JC, Barkowitz P: Do "they all look alike"? The effect of race, sex, experience, and attitudes on the ability to recognize faces. Journal of Applied Social Psychology 1978; 8:306-318

Brigham JC, Bothwell RK: The ability of prospective jurors to estimate the accuracy of eyewitness identifications. Law and Human Behavior 1983; 7:19-30

Brigham JC, Cairns, DL: The effect of mugshot inspections on eyewitness identification accuracy. Journal of Applied Social Psychology 1988; 18:1394-1410

Brigham JC, Maass A, Martinez D, Whittenberger G: The effect of arousal on facial recognition. Basic & Applied Social Psychology 1983; 4:279-293

Brigham JC, Maass A, Snyder LS, Spaulding K: The accuracy of eyewitness identifications in a field setting. Journal of Personality and Social Psychology 1982; 42:673-681

Brigham JC, Pfeifer JE: Evaluating the fairness of lineups, in Adult Eyewitness Testimony: Current Trends and Developments. Edited by Ross DF, Read JD, Toglia MP, New York, Cambridge University Press, 1994

Brigham JC, Ready DJ: Own-race bias in lineup construction. Law and Human Behavior 1985; 9:415-424

Brigham JC, Van Verst M, Bothwell RK: Accuracy of children's eyewitness identifications in a field setting. Basic and Applied Social Psychology 1986; 7:295-306

Brigham JC, Wolfskeil MP: Opinions of attorneys and law enforcement personnel on the accuracy of eyewitness identification. Law and Human Behavior 1983; 7:337-349

Brodsky SL: Testifying in Court: Guidelines and Maxims for the Expert Witness. Washington, DC, American Psychological Association, 1991

Brown EL, Deffenbacher KA, Sturgill W: Memory for faces and the circumstances of encounter. Journal of Applied Psychology 1977; 62:311-318

Brown R, Kulik J: Flashbulb memories. Cognition 1977; 5: 73-99

Bruner J, Postman L, Rodrigues J: Expectation and the perception of color. American Journal of Psychology 1951; 64:216-227

Buckhout R, Alper A, Chern S, Silverberg G, Slomovits M: Determinants of eyewitness performance on a lineup. Bulletin of the Psychonomic Society 1974; 4:191-192

Buckhout R, Figueroa D, Hoff E: Eyewitness identification: effects of suggestion and bias in identification from photographs. Bulletin of the Psychonomic Society 1975; 6:71-74

Buckhout R: Double mistaken identification in Dallas: Texas v. Lenell Geter and Anthony Williams. Social Action and the Law 1984; 10:3-11

Buckhout R: Eyewitness memory. Scientific American 1974; 231:23-31

Buckhout R: Nearly 2,000 witnesses can be wrong. Bulletin of the Psychonomic Society 1980; 16:307-310

Bull RHC, Green J: The relationship between physical appearance and criminality. Medical Science and Law 1980; 20:79-83

Carson D: Professionals and the courts. Birmingham, UK, Venture Press, 1990

Ceci SJ, Bruck M: Suggestibility of the child witness: a historical review and synthesis. Psychological Bulletin 1993; 113:403-439

Ceci SJ, Ross DF, Toglia MP: Perspectives on Children's Testimony. New York, Springer-Verlag, 1989

Ceci SJ, Toglia MP, Ross DF (Eds.): Children's Eyewitness Memory. New York, Springer-Verlag 1987

Champagne A, Shuman D, Whitaker E: Expert witness in courts: an empirical examination. Judicature 1992; 76:5-10

Chance J, Goldstein AG, McBride L: Differential experience and recognition memory for faces. Journal of Social Psychology 1975; 97:243-253

Chen YY, Geiselman RE: Effects of ethnic stereotyping and ethnically-related cognitive biases on eyewitness recollections of height. American Journal of Forensic Psychology 1993;11:2:13-19

Christiaansen RE, Ochalek K, Sweeney D: Individual differences in eyewitness memory and confidence judgments. Journal of General Psychology 1984; 110:47-52

Christiaansen RE, Sweeney JD, Ochalek K: Influencing eyewitness descriptions. Law and Human Behavior 1983; 7:59-65

Christianson S-A, Hubinette B: Hands up! A study of witnesses' emotional reactions and memories associated with bank robberies. Applied Cognitive Psychology 1993; 7:365-380

Christianson S-A, Loftus EF: Memory for traumatic events. Applied Cognitive Psychology 1987; 1:225-239

Christianson S-A, Loftus EF: Remembering emotional events: the fate of detailed information. Cognition & Emotion 1991; 5:2:81-108

Christianson S-A: Emotional stress and eyewitness memory: a critical review. Psychological Bulletin 1992; 112: 284-309

Cialdini RB: Influence: Science and Practice. Glenview, IL, Scott, Foresman/Little Brown, 1988

Clifford BR, Davies G: Procedures for obtaining identification evidence, in Psychological Methods in Criminal Investigation and Evidence. Edited by Raskin D. New York, Springer 1989; 47-95

Clifford BR, Hollin CR: Effects of the type of incident and the number of perpetrators on eyewitness memory. Journal of Applied Psychology 1981; 66:364-370

Clifford BR, Scott J: Individual and situational factors in eyewitness testimony. Journal of Applied Psychology 1978; 63:352-359

Clifford BR: Police as eyewitnesses. New Society 1976; 36:176-177

Cohen G, Faulkner D: Age differences in source forgetting: effects on reality monitoring and on eyewitness testimony. Psychology and Aging 1989; 4:10-17

Comish S: Recognition of facial stimuli following an intervening task involving the Identi-kit. Journal of Applied Psychology 1987; 72:488-491

Cooke D: Do I feel lucky? Survival in the witness box. Neuropsychology 1990; 4:271-285

Corder BF, Spalding V, Whiteside JD, Whiteside R: Expert witness testimony in sentencing phases of trials: survey of judges, attorneys, psychiatrists, and psychologists. American Journal of Forensic Psychology 1990; 8:55-62

Cutler BL, Berman GL, Penrod S, Fisher RP: Conceptual, practical, and empirical issues associated with eyewitness identification test media, in Adult Eyewitness Testimony: Current Trends and Developments. Edited by Ross DF, Read JD, Toglia MP. New York, Cambridge University Press, 1994

Cutler BL, Dexter HR, Penrod SD: Expert testimony and jury decision making: an empirical analysis. Behavioral Sciences and Law 1989; 7:215-225

Cutler BL, Dexter HR, Penrod SD: Nonadversarial methods for sensitizing jurors to eyewitness evidence. Journal of Applied Social Psychology 1990; 20:14 Pt 2:1197-1207

Cutler BL, Penrod SD, Dexter HR: The eyewitness, the expert psychologist, and the jury. Law & Human Behavior 1989; 13:3:311-332

Cutler BL, Penrod SD, Martens TK: The reliability of eyewitness identification: the role of system and estimator variables. Law and Human Behavior 1987; 11:233-258

Cutler BL, Penrod SD: Improving the reliability of eyewitness identification: lineup construction and presentation. Journal of Applied Psychology 1988; 73:281-290

Cutler BL, Penrod SD: Mistaken Identification: The Eyewitness, Psychology, and the Law. New York, Cambridge University Press, 1995

Cutler BL, Penrod SD: Moderators of the confidence-accuracy correlation in face recognition: the role of information processing and base rates. Applied Cognitive Psychology 1989; 3:95-107

Daubert v. Merrell Dow Pharmaceuticals, 113 S. Ct. 2786 (1993)

Davies GM, Ellis HD, Shepherd JW (Eds.): Perceiving and Remembering Faces. London, Academic Press, 1981

Davies GM, Shepherd JW, Ellis HD: Effects of interpolated mugshot exposure on accuracy of eyewitness identification. Journal of Applied Psychology 1979; 64: 232-237

Davies GM: Influencing public policy in eyewitnessing: problems and possibilities, in Psychology and Law. Edited by Losel F, Bender D, Bliesener T. deGruyter, Berlin, 1992; 265-274

Deffenbacher K, Carr TH, Leu JR: Memory for words, pictures, and faces: retroactive interference, forgetting and reminiscence. Journal of Experimental Psychology: Human Learning and Memory 1981; 7:299-305

Deffenbacher KA, Cross JF, Handkins RE, Chance, JE, et al.: Relevance of voice identification research to criteria for evaluating reliability of an identification. Journal of Psychology 1989; 123:109-119

Deffenbacher KA, Loftus EF: Do jurors share a common understanding concerning eyewitness behavior? Law & Human Behavior 1982; 6:15-30

Deffenbacher KA: A maturing of research on the behavior of eyewitnesses. Applied Cognitive Psychology 1991; 5:5: 377-402

Deffenbacher KA: Effects of arousal on everyday memory. Special issue: State-dependent cognitive functioning: I. Human Performance 1994; 7:141-161

Deffenbacher KA: Experimental psychology actually can assist triers of fact. American Psychologist 1984; 39: 9:1066-1068

Deffenbacher KA: Eyewitness accuracy and confidence: can we infer anything about their relationship? Law and Human Behavior 1980; 4:243-260

Deffenbacher KA: The influence of arousal on reliability of testimony, in Evaluating Witness Evidence. Edited by Lloyd-Bostock SMA, Clifford BR. Chichester, John Wiley 1983; 235-251

Deffenbacher KA, Brown EL, Sturgill W: Some predictors of eyewitness memory accuracy, in Practical Aspects of Memory. Edited by Gruneberg MM, Morris PE, Sykes RN. London, Academic Press 1978; 219-226

Deffenbacher KA: On the memorability of the human face, in Aspects of Face Processing. Edited by Ellis HD, Newcombe JF, Young A. Dordrecht, Netherlands, Martinus Nijhoff 1986; 61-70

Dershowitz, AM: The Abuse Excuse. New York, Little Brown, 1994

Devlin Lord: Report to the Secretary of State for the Home Department of the Departmental Committee on Evidence of Identification in Criminal Cases. London, Her Majesty's Stationary Office, 1976

Diamond SS: Using psychology to control law: from deceptive advertising to criminal sentencing. Law and Human Behavior 1989; 13:239-252

Diges M: Stereotypes and memory of real traffic accidents, in Practical Aspects of Memory: Current Research and Issues, Volume I. Edited by Gruneburg MM, Morris PE, Sykes RN. Chichester, Wiley, 1988; 59-65

Dodd DH, Bradshaw J: Leading questions and memory: pragmatic constraints. Journal of Verbal Learning and Verbal Behavior 1980; 19:695-704

Domingo F: Survey to study the feasibility of conducting a national composite artist conference. Unpublished report, City of New York Police Department, 1984

Doob AN, Kirshenbaum H: Bias in police lineups—partial remembering. Journal of Police Science and Administration 1973; 1:287-293

Doyle JM: Applying lawyer's expertise to scientific experts: some thoughts about trial court analysis of the prejudicial effects of admitting and excluding expert scientific testimony. Wm. & Mary Law Review 1984; 25:619:647-648

Easterbrook JA: The effect of emotion on the utilization and organization of behavior. Psychological Review 1959; 66:183-201.

Egan D, Pittner M, Goldstein AG: Eyewitness identification: photographs vs. line models. Law and Human Behavior 1977; 11:199-206

Egeth H: Expert psychological testimony about eyewitnesses: an update, in Psychology, Science, and Human Affairs: Essays in Honor of William Bevan. Edited by Kessel F. Boulder, CO, Westview Press, 1995

Egeth HE: What do we not know about eyewitness identification? American Psychologist 1993; 48:577-580

Ellis HD, Davies GM, McMurran, MM: Recall of white and black faces by white and black witnesses using the Photofit system. Human Factors 1979; 21:1:55-59

Ellison KW, Buckhout R: Psychology and Criminal Justice. New York, Harper & Row, 1981

Eysenck MW: A Handbook of Cognitive Psychology. Hillsdale, NJ, Erlbaum, 1984

Eysenck MW: Human Memory: Theory, Research and Individual Differences. New York, Pergamon Press, 1977

Farrington DP, Lambert S: Predictive violence and burglary offenders from victim, witness and offense data. Paper presented to the First NISCALE workshop on criminality and law enforcement, The Hague, Netherlands, 1993

Federal Rules of Evidence for United States Courts and Magistrates. St. Paul, MN, West Publishing, 1975

Ferman S, Entwistle DR: Children's ability to recognize other children's faces. Child Development 1976; 47:506-510

Festinger L, Carlsmith JM: Cognitive consequences of forced compliance. Journal of Abnormal and Social Psychology 1959; 58:203-210

Fischhoff B: Hindsight does not equal foresight: the effect of outcome knowledge on judgment under uncertainty. Journal of Experimental Psychology: Human Perception and Performance 1975; 1:288-299

Fisher RP, Geiselman RE, Amador M: Field tests of the cognitive interview: enhancing the recollection of actual victims and witnesses of crime. Journal of Applied Psychology 1989; 74:722-727

Fisher RP, Geiselman RE: Memory Enhancing Techniques for Investigative Interviewing. Springfield, IL, Charles Thomas Publishers, 1992

Foster RA, Libkuman TM, Schooler JW, Loftus EF: Consequentiality and eyewitness person identification. Applied Cognitive Psychology 1994; 8:107-121

Frazzetti AE, Toland K, Teller SA, Loftus EF: Memory and eyewitness testimony, in Aspects of Memory. Edited by Gruneburg MM, Morris PE. London, Routledge, 1992; 18-50

Freckelton I: Science and the legal culture. Expert Evidence 1993; 2:107-114

Frye v. United States, 293 F 1013 34 ALR 145 (DC Cir., 1923)

Galper RE: "Functional race membership" and recognition of faces. Perceptual and Motor Skills 1973; 37:455-462

Gary M, Loftus EF, Brown, SW: Memory: a river runs through it. Consciousness and Cognition 1994; 3:438-451

Geiselman RE, Fisher RP, Cohen G, Holland H, et al.: Eyewitness responses to leading and misleading questions under the cognitive interview. Journal of Police Science & Administration 1986; 14:1:31-39

Geiselman RE, Fisher RP, MacKinnon DP, Holland HL: Enhancement of eyewitness memory with the cognitive interview. American Journal of Psychology 1986; 99:385-401

Geiselman RE, Fisher RP: Ten years of cognitive interviewing, in A Synthesis of Basic and Applied Approaches to Human Memory. Edited by Payne DG, Conrad FG. New York, Lawrence Earlbaum, 1996

Geiselman RE, Haghighi D, Stown R: Unconscious transference and characteristics of accurate and inaccurate eyewitnesses. Psychology, Crime, and Law 1995; 2:131-141

Geiselman RE, MacArthur A, Meerovitch S: Transference of perpetrator roles in eyewitness identification from photoarrays. American Journal of Forensic Psychology 1993; 11:4:5-15

Goldstein AG, Chance JE, Schneller GR: Frequency of eyewitness identification in criminal cases: a survey of prosecutors. Bulletin of the Psychonomic Society 1989; 27:71-74

Gonzalez R, Ellsworth PC, Pembroke M: Response biases in lineups and showups Journal of Personality and Social Psychology 1993; 64:525-537

Goodman GS, Bottoms BL (Eds.): Child Victims, Child Witnesses: Understanding and Improving Testimony. New York, Guilford Press, 1993

Gorenstein GW, Ellsworth PC: Effect of choosing an incorrect photograph on a later identification by an eyewitness. Journal of Applied Psychology 1980; 65:616-622

Green DL, Geiselman RE: Building composite facial images: effects of feature saliency and delay of construction. Journal of Applied Psychology 1989; 74:5:714-721

Greene EJ: Judge's instruction on eyewitness testimony: evaluation and revision. Journal of Applied Social Psychology 1988; 18:3:252-276

Haghighi D, Geiselman RE: Identifying Perpetrators of Classroom Disruptions. University of California, Los Angeles, Unpublished Honors Thesis, 1996

Hall DF, Ostrom TM: Accuracy of eyewitness identification after biased or unbiased instructions. Unpublished (Ohio State University), 1975

Hall DF: Obtaining eyewitness identifications in criminal investigations: applications of social and experimental psychology (Doctoral dissertation, Ohio State University, Columbus, 1976). Dissertation Abstracts International, 37:2569B

Hastie R, Landsman R, Loftus EF: Eyewitness testimony: the dangers of guessing. Jurimetrics Journal 1978; 19:1-8

Hastie R, Penrod, SD, Pennington N: Inside the Jury. Cambridge, MA, Harvard University Press, 1983

Hastie R: Notes on the psychologist expert witness. Law and Human Behavior 1986; 10:79-82

Herbert DL, Barrett RK: Attorney's Master Guide to Courtroom Psychology: How to Apply Behavioral Science Techniques for New Trial Success. Englewood Cliffs, NJ, Executive Reports Corp., 1980

Hollin CR, Clifford BR: Eyewitness testimony: the effects of discussion on recall accuracy and agreement. Journal of Applied Social Psychology 1983; 13:234-244

Holst VF, Pezdek K: Scripts for typical crimes and their effects on memory for eyewitness testimony. Applied Cognitive Psychology 1992; 6:7:573-587

Hosch HM, Beck EL, McIntyre P: Influence of expert testimony regarding eyewitness accuracy on jury decisions. Law and Human Behavior 1980; 4:287-296

Hosch HM, Bothwell RK: Arousal, description and identification accuracy of victims and bystanders. Journal of Social Behavior & Personality 1990; 5:5:481-488

Hosch HM, Cooper, DS: Victimization as a determinant of eyewitness accuracy. Journal of Applied Psychology 1982; 67:649-652

Hosch HM, Leippe MR, Marchioni PM, Cooper, DS: Victimization, self-monitoring, and eyewitness identification. Journal of Applied Psychology 1984; 69:280-288

Hosch HM, Platz SJ: Self-monitoring and eyewitness accuracy. Personality and Social Psychology Bulletin 1984; 10:289-292

Houts M: From Evidence to Guilt. Springfield, IL, Charles Thomas, 1956

Huff R, Rattner A, Sagarin E: Guilty until proven innocent. Crime and Delinquency 1986; 32:518-544

James W: Principles of Psychology. New York, Holt, 1890

Jenkins F, Davies GM: Contamination of facial memory through exposure to misleading composite pictures. Journal of Applied Psychology 1985; 70:164-176

Johnson MK, Raye CL: Reality monitoring. Psychological Review 1981; 88:67-85

Kahneman D: Attention and Effort. London, Prentice-Hall, 1973

Kalven H, Zeisel H: The American Jury. Boston, Little, Brown, 1966

Kassin SM, Barndollar KA: The psychology of eyewitness testimony: a comparison of experts and prospective jurors. Journal of Applied Social Psychology 1992; 22:16:1241-1249

Kassin SM, Ellsworth PC, Smith VL: Deja vu all over again: Elliott's critique of eyewitness experts. Law and Human Behavior 1994; 18:203-210

Kassin SM: Eyewitness identification: victims versus bystanders. Journal of Applied Social Psychology 1984; 14:519-529

Kelley CM, Lindsay SD: Remembering mistaken for knowing: ease of retrieval as a basis for confidence in answers to general knowledge questions. Journal of Memory & Language 1993; 32:1:1-24.

Kennedy TD, Haygood RC: The discrediting effect in eyewitness testimony. Journal of Applied Social Psychology 1992; 22:70-82

Kirby v. Illinois, 406 US 682, 32 L Ed 2d 411, 92 S Ct 1877 (1972)

Koehnken G, Maass A: Eyewitness testimony: False alarms on biased instructions? Journal of Applied Psychology 1988; 73:363-370

Koehnken G, Maass A: Realism, reactance, and instructional bias in eyewitness identification, in Social/Ecological Psychology and the Psychology of Women. Edited by Denmark FL. Amsterdam, North Holland, 1985

Konecni VJ, Ebbesen EB: Courtroom testimony by psychologists on eyewitness identification issues: critical notes and reflections. Law and Human Behavior 1986; 10:117-126

Koriat A: Memory's knowledge of its own knowledge: the accessibility account of the feeling of knowing, in Metacognition: Knowing About Knowing. Edited by Metcalfe J, Shimamura AP. Cambridge, MA, MIT Press, 1994

Krafka C, Penrod SD: Reinstatement of context in a field experiment on eyewitness identification. Journal of Personality and Social Psychology 1985; 49:58-69

Kramer TH, Buckhout R, Eugenio P: Weapon focus, arousal, and eyewitness memory. Law and Human Behavior 1990; 14:167-184

Kramer TH, Buckhout R, Fox P, Widman E, et al.: Effects of stress on recall. Applied Cognitive Psychology 1991; 5:483-488

Lavrakas PJ, Buri JR, Mayzner MS: A perspective on the recognition of other race faces. Perception and Psychophysics 1976; 20:475-481

Lee T, Geiselman RE: Recall of perpetrator height as a function of eyewitness and perpetrator ethnicity. Psychology, Crime & Law 1994; 1:1-9

Leippe MR: Effects of integrative memorial and cognitive processes on the correspondence of eyewitness accuracy and confidence. Law and Human Behavior 1980; 4:261-274

Lempert RO: Social sciences in court: on "eyewitness experts" and other issues. Law and Human Behavior 1896; 10:167-182

Levine RI, Tapp JL: The psychology of criminal identification: the gap from Wade to Kirby. University of Pennsylvania Law Review 1973; 212:1079

Lindsay DS: Eyewitness suggestibility. Current Directions in Psychological Science 1993; 2:86-89

Lindsay DS: Memory source monitoring and eyewitness testimony, in Adult Eyewitness Testimony: Current Trends and Developments. Edited by Ross DF, Read JD, Toglia MP. New York, Cambridge University Press, 1994

Lindsay RC, Wells GL, Rumpel CM: Can people detect eyewitness-identification accuracy within and across situations? Journal of Applied Psychology 1981; 66:776-784.

Lindsay RCL, Harvie VL: Hits, false alarms, correct and mistaken identifications: the effect of method of data collection on facial memory, in Practical Aspects of Memory: Current Research and Issues. Edited by Gruneberg MM, Morris PE, Sykes RN. Chichester, Wiley, 1988

Lindsay RCL, Lea JA, Fulford JA: Sequential lineup presentation: technique matters. Journal of Applied Psychology 1991; 76:741-745

Lindsay RCL, Martin R, Webber L: Default values in eyewitness descriptions: a problem for the match-to-description lineup foil selection strategy. Law & Human Behavior 1994; 18:527-541

Lindsay RCL, Nosworthy GJ, Martin R, Martynuck C: Using mugshots to find suspects. Journal of Applied Psychology 1994; 79:121-130

Lindsay RCL, Wells GL, O'Connor FJ: Mock juror belief of accurate and inaccurate eyewitnesses: a replication and extension. Law and Human Behavior 1989; 13:333-339

Lindsay RCL, Wells GL, Rumpel CM: Can people detect eyewitness identification accuracy within and across situations? Journal of Applied Psychology 1981; 66:79-89

Lindsay RCL, Wells GL: Improving eyewitness identifications from lineups: simultaneous versus sequential lineup presentation. Journal of Applied Psychology 1985; 70:556-564

Lindsay RCL, Wells GL: What do we really know about cross-race eyewitness identification? in Evaluating Witness Evidence: Recent Psychological Research and New Perspectives. Edited by Lloyd-Bostock S, Clifford BR. Chichester, UK, Wiley, 1983; 219-233

Lindsay RCL, Wells GL: What price justice? Exploring the relationship of lineup fairness to identification accuracy. Law and Human Behavior 1980; 4:303-314

Lindsay RCL: Biased lineups: Where do they come from? in Adult Eyewitness Testimony: Current Trends and Developments. Edited by Ross DF, Read JD, Toglia MP. New York, Cambridge University Press, 1994

Lindsay RCL: Expectations of eyewitness performance: jurors' verdicts do not follow from their beliefs, in Adult Eyewitness Testimony: Current Trends and Developments. Edited by Ross DF, Read JD, Toglia MP. New York, Cambridge University Press, 1994

Lisko KO: Juror perceptions of witness credibility as a function of linguistic and nonverbal power. Dissertation Abstracts International 1993; 54:2-A:371

List JA: Age and schematic differences in the reliability of eyewitness testimony. Developmental Psychology 1986; 22:50-57

Loftus EF, Burns TE: Mental shock can produce retrograde amnesia. Memory and Cognition 1982; 10:318-323

Loftus EF, Donders K, Hoffman HG, Schooler JW: Creating new memories that are quickly accessed and confidently held. Memory and Cognition 1989; 17:607-616

Loftus EF, Greene E: Warning: even memory for faces may be contagious. Law and Human Behavior 1980; 4:323-334

Loftus EF, Hoffman HG: Misinformation and memory: the creation of new memories. Journal of Experimental Psychology: General 1989; 118:100-104

Loftus EF, Kaufman L: Why do traumatic experiences sometimes produce good memory (flashbulbs) and sometimes no memory (repression)? in Affect and Accuracy in Recall: Cognition. Edited by Winograd E, Neisser U. New York, Cambridge University Press, 1993; 212-223

Loftus EF, Ketcham K: Witness for the Defense. New York, St. Martins Press, 1991

Loftus EF, Levidow B, Duensing S; Who remembers best? Individual differences in memory for events that occurred in a science museum. Applied Cognitive Psychology 1992; 6:93-107

Loftus EF, Loftus GR, Messo J: Some facts about "weapon focus." Law and Human Behavior 1987; 11:55-62

Loftus EF, Loftus GR: On the permanence of stored information in the human brain. American Psychologist 1980; 35:409-420

Loftus EF, Miller DG, Burns HG: Semantic integration of verbal information into visual memory. Journal of Experimental Psychology: Human Learning and Memory 1978; 4:19-31

Loftus EF, Palmer JE: Reconstruction of automobile destruction: an example of the interaction between language and memory. Journal of Verbal Learning and Verbal Behavior 1974; 13:585-589

Loftus EF, Schooler JW, Boone SM, Kline D: Time went by so slowly: overestimation of event duration by males and females. Applied Cognitive Psychology 1987; 1:3-13

Loftus EF, Zanni G: Eyewitness testimony: the influence of the wording of a question. Bulletin of the Psychonomic Society 1975; 5:86-88

Loftus EF: Eyewitness Testimony. Cambridge, MA, Harvard University Press, 1979

Loftus EF: Impact of expert psychological testimony on the unreliability of eyewitness identification. Journal of Applied Psychology 1980; 65:1:9-15

Loftus EF: Unconscious transference in eyewitness identification. Law and Psychology Review 1976; 2:93-98

Loftus EF: When a lie becomes memory's truth: memory distortion after exposure to misinformation. Current Directions in Psychological Science 1992; 1:4:121-123

Loftus GR, Mackworth NH: Cognitive determinants of fixation location during picture viewing. Journal of Experimental Psychology: Human Perception & Performance 1978; 4:4:565-572

Luce T: Blacks, whites, yellows: they all look alike to me. Psychology Today 1974; 8:105-108

Luus CAE, Wells GL: Eyewitness identification and the selection of distractors for lineups. Law and Human Behavior 1991; 15:43-57

Luus CAE, Wells GL: Eyewitness identification confidence, in Adult Eyewitness Testimony: Current Trends and Developments. Edited by Ross DF, Read JD, Toglia MP. New York, Cambridge University Press, 1994

Luus CAE, Wells GL: The malleability of eyewitness confidence: co-witness and perseverance effects. Journal of Applied Psychology 1994; 79:714-723

Luus CAE: Eyewitness confidence: social influence and belief perseverance. Unpublished doctoral dissertation, Iowa State University, 1991

Maass A, Brigham JC, West SG: Testifying on eyewitness reliability: expert advice is not always persuasive. Journal of Applied Social Psychology 1985; 15:207-229

Maass A, Kohnken G: Eyewitness identification: simulating the 'weapon effect.' Law and Human Behavior 1989; 13:397-408

MacLeod MD, Frowley JN, Shepherd JW: Whole body information: its relevance to eyewitnesses, in Adult Eyewitness Testimony: Current Trends and Developments. Edited by Ross DF, Read JD, Toglia MP. New York, Cambridge University Press, 1994

Malpass RS, Devine PG: Guided memory in eyewitness identification. Journal of Applied Psychology 1981; 66:343-350

Malpass RS, Devine PG: Measuring the fairness of eyewitness identification lineups, in Evaluating Witness Evidence. Edited by Lloyd-Bostock SMA, Clifford BR. London, John Wiley & Sons, 1983

Malpass RS, Devine PG: Realism and eyewitness identification research. Law and Human Behavior 1980; 4:347-358

Malpass RS, Kravitz J: Recognition for faces of own and other race. Journal of Personality and Social Psychology 1969; 13:330-334

Malpass RS: Differential recognition for faces of own and other race: a data summary paper presented at the meeting of the Academy of Criminal Justice Sciences, Louisville Kentucky, 1982

Manson v. Brathwaite, 432 U.S. 98, 112, 97 S. Ct. 2243, 2252, 53 L.Ed.2d 140 (1977).

Mantwill M, Koehnken G, Aschermann E: Effects of the cognitive interview on the recall of familiar and unfamiliar events. Journal of Applied Psychology 1995; 80:68-78

Mauldin M, Laughery K: Composite production effects upon subsequential facial recognition. Journal of Applied Psychology 1981; 66:351-357

McAllister HA, Dale RH, Keay CE: Effects of lineup modality on witness credibility. Journal of Social Psychology 1993; 133:365-376

McCloskey M, Egeth H, McKenna J: The experimental psychologist in court: the ethics of expert testimony. Law and Human Behavior 1986; 10:1-14

McCloskey M, Egeth H: Eyewitness identification: what can a psychologist tell a jury? American Psychologist 1983; 38:550-563

McCloskey M, Zaragoza M: Misleading post-event information and memory for events: arguments and evidence against the memory impairment hypothesis. Journal of Experimental Psychology 1985; 114:1-16

McKenna J, Treadway M, McCloskey ME: Expert psychological testimony on eyewitness reliability: selling psychology before its time, in Psychology and Social Policy. Edited by Suedfeld P, Tetlock PE. New York, Hemisphere Publishing Corp, 1992

Meier P: Damned liars and expert witnesses. Presidential Address, American Statistical Association, Annual Meeting, 1982

Mello EW, Fisher RP: Enhancing elderly eyewitness memory with the cognitive interview. Paper presented at the annual meeting of the American Psychological Association. New York, August, 1995

Melton GB: Bringing psychology to the legal system: opportunities, obstacles, and efficacy. American Psychologist 1987; 42:488-495

Melton GB: Expert opinions: "Not for cosmic understanding." Psychology in Litigation and Legislation. Edited by Sales BD, VandenBos GR. Washington, DC, American Psychological Association, 1995; 59-99

Memon A, Dionne R, Short L, Maralani S, MacKinnon D, Geiselman RE: Psychological factors in the use of photospreads. Journal of Police Science and Administration 1988; 16:62-69

Monahan J, Loftus EF: The psychology of law. Annual Review of Psychology 1982; 33:441-475

Moore PJ: Eyewitness testimony in actual criminal cases: a multi-method approach to evaluating current theory and research. Dissertation Abstracts International 1993; 53:11-B:6041

Moore v. Illinois, 434 U.S. 220 (1977)

Munsterberg H: On the Witness Stand: Essays on Psychology and Crime. New York, Doubleday, 1908

Murray DM, Wells GL: Does knowledge that a crime was staged affect eyewitness performance? Journal of Applied Social Psychology 1982; 12:42-53

Narby DJ, Cutler BL: Effectiveness of voir dire as a safeguard in eyewitness cases. Journal of Applied Psychology 1994; 79:724-729

Navon D: Selection of lineup foils by similarity to suspect is likely to misfire. Law and Human Behavior 1992; 16:575-593

Neil v. Biggers, 409 U.S. 188, 93 S. Ct. 375; 34 L. Ed. 2d 401 (1972)

Neisser U, Harsch N: Phantom flashbulbs: false recollections of hearing the news about Challenger, in Affect and Accuracy in Recall: Studies of "Flashbulb" Memories. Edited by Winograd E, Neisser U. Cambridge, Cambridge University Press, 1992

Ng W, Lindsay RCL: Cross-race facial recognition: failure of the contact hypothesis. Journal of Cross-Cultural Psychology 1994; 25:217-232

Nisbett R, Ross L: Human inference: strategies and shortcomings of social judgment. Englewood Cliffs, NJ. Prentice-Hall, 1980

Norman DA, Rumelhart DE: The LNR approach to human information processing. Cognition 1981; 10:1-3:235-240

O'Barr WM: Linguistic Evidence: Language, Power, and Strategy in the Courtroom. New York, Academic Press, 1982

O'Rourke TE, Penrod SD, Culter BL, Stuve TE: The external validity of eyewitness identification research: generalizing across age groups. Law and Human Behavior 1989; 13:385-397

O'Toole AJ, Deffenbacher KA, Valentin D, Abdi H: Structural aspects of face recognition and the other-race effect. Memory & Cognition 1994; 22, 208-224

Paley B, Geiselman RE: The effects of alternative photospread instructions on suspect identification performance. American Journal of Forensic Psychology 1989; 7:3-13

Penrod SD, Fulero SM, Cutler BL: Expert psychological testimony on eyewitness reliability before and after Daubert: the state of the law and the science. Behavioral Science and the Law 1995; 13:1-15

People v. Blair, 25 Cal. ed 143, 148-149 (1979)

People v. Brandon, 32 Cal. App. 4th 1033 (1995)

People v. Faulkner, 28 Cal. App. 3d 384, 390 (1972)

People v. Gaglione, 26 Cal App 4th 1291, 32 Cal Rptr 2d 169 (July, 1994)

People v. Guzman, 47 Cal. App. 3d 380, 121 Cal. Rptr. 69 (1975)

People v. Holt, 28 Cal. App. 3d 343, 349-350 (1982)

People v. Johnson, 38 Cal. App. 3d 1, 112 Cal. Rptr. 834 (1974)

People v. Leahy, 94 Daily Journal D.A.R. 15165 (1994)

People v. Lewis, 520 N.Y.S.2d 125 (1987)

People v. McDonald, 208 Cal. Rptr. 236, 690 P.2d 709 (California, 1984)

People v. Perkins, 184 Cal. App. 3d 583, 589 (1986)

People v. Sandoval, 30 Cal App 4th 1288, 36 Cal Rptr 2d 646 (November, 1994)

People v. Shirley, 31 Cal. 3d 18, 641 P. 2d 775, 181 Cal. Rptr. 243 (1982) reh'g denied June 4, 1982

People v. Thomas, 5 Cal. App. 3d 889, 900 (1970)

People v. Wimberly, 7 Cal. App. 2d 152 (1992)

Peters DP: Eyewitness memory and arousal in a natural setting, in Practical Aspects of Memory: Current Research and Issues. Memory in Everyday Life. Edited by Gruneberg MM, Morris PE, Sykes RN. Chichester, John Wiley, 1988; 89-94

Pickel KL: Evaluation and integration of eyewitness reports. Law and Human Behavior 1993; 17:569-595.

Pigott M, Brigham JC: Relationship between accuracy of prior description and facial recognition. Journal of Applied Psychology 1985; 70:547-555

Platz SJ, Hosch HM: Cross-racial/ethnic eyewitness identification: a field study. Journal of Applied Social Psychology 1988; 18:11:972-984

Powers PA, Andriks JL, Loftus EF: Eyewitness accounts of females and males. Journal of Applied Psychology 1979; 64:339-347

Ramirez G, Zemba D, Geiselman RE: Judges' cautionary instructions on eyewitness testimony. American Journal of Forensic Psychology 1996; 14:1:31-66

Rand Corporation: The Criminal Investigation Process, Volumes 1-3. Rand Corporation Technical Report R-1776-DOJ, R-1777-DOJ. Santa Monica, CA, 1975

Rattner A: Convicted but innocent. Law and Human Behavior 1988; 12:283-293

Read JD, Tollestrup P, Hammersley R, McFadzen E, Christensen A: The unconscious transference effect: are innocent bystanders ever misidentified? Applied Cognitive Psychology 1990; 4:3-31

Read JD, Vokey JR, Hammersley R: Changing photos of faces: effects of exposure duration and photo similarity on recognition and the accuracy-confidence relationship. Journal of Experimental Psychology: Learning, Memory, and Cognition 1990; 16:870-882.

Read JD, Yuille JC, Tollestrup P: Recollections of a robbery: effects of arousal and alcohol upon recall and person identification. Law and Human Behavior 1992; 16:425-446.

Read JD: The availability heuristic in person identification: the sometimes misleading consequences of enhanced contextual information. Applied Cognitive Psychology 1995; 9:91-121

Read JD: Understanding bystander misidentifications: the role of familiarity and contextual knowledge, in Adult Eyewitness Testimony: Current Trends and Developments. Edited by Ross DF, Read JD, Toglia MP. New York, Cambridge University Press, 1994

Reynolds JK, Pezdek K: Face recognition memory: the effects of exposure duration and encoding instruction. Applied Cognitive Psychology 1992; 6:279-292

Reynolds JK, Pezdek K: Face recognition memory: the effects of exposure duration and encoding instructions. Applied Cognitive Psychology 1992; 6:279-292.

Rhodes G, Tan S, Brake S, Taylor K: Expertise and configural coding in face recognition. British Journal of Psychology 1989; 80:313-331

Ross DF, Ceci SJ, Dunning D, Toglia MP: Unconscious transference and lineup identification: toward a memory blending approach, in Adult Eyewitness Testimony: Current Trends and Developments. Edited by Ross DF, Read JD, Toglia MP. New York, Cambridge University Press, 1994

Rupp A, Warmbrand A, Karash A, Buckhout R: Effects of group interaction on eyewitness reports. Paper presented at the meetings of the Eastern Psychological Association, New York, 1976

Ryan RH, Geiselman RE: Effects of biased information on the relationship between eyewitness confidence and accuracy. Bulletin of the Psychonomic Society 1991; 29:1:7-9

Saks MJ, Hastie R: Social Psychology in Court. New York, Van Nostrand Reinhold, 1978

Saks MJ: Expert witnesses, nonexpert witnesses, and nonwitness experts. Annual Meeting of the American Psychological Association: American Psychology-Law Society Presidential Address: Expert witnesses: Psychology and Law & Human Behavior 1990; 14:4:291-313

Sales BD, Shuman, DW: Reclaiming the integrity of science in expert witnessing. Special issue: The ethics of expert witnessing. Ethics & Behavior 1993; 3:223-229

Sanders GS: On increasing the usefulness of eyewitness research. Law and Human Behavior 1986; 10:333-336

Saywitz K, Geiselman RE: Techniques for maximizing completeness while minimizing errors in children's recall of events, in Truth and Memory. Edited by Lynn S. New York, Guilford, in press

Schneider AL, Griffith WR, Sumi DH, Burcart JM: Portland Forward Records Check of Crime Victims. Washington, D.C, U.S. Department of Justice, 1987

Schooler JW, Engstler-Schooler TY: Verbal overshadowing of visual memories: some things are better left unsaid. Cognitive Psychology 1990; 17:36-71

Schulster J: Phenomenological correlates of a self theory of memory. American Journal of Psychology 1981; 94:527-537

Scogin F, Calhoon SK, E'Errico M: Eyewitness confidence and accuracy among three age cohorts. Journal of Applied Gerontology 1994; 13:172-184

Shapiro PN, Penrod SD: Meta-analysis of face identification studies. Psychological Bulletin 1986; 100:139-156

Shaw JI, Skolnick P: Sex differences, weapon focus, and eyewitness reliability. Journal of Social Psychology 1994; 134:413-420

Shepherd JW, Deregowski JB: Races and faces—a comparison of the responses of Africans and Europeans to faces of the same and different races. British Journal of Social Psychology 1981; 20:125-133

Shuman DW, Whitaker E, Champagne A: An empirical examination of the use of expert witnesses in the courts—Part II: A three city study. Jurimetrics 1994; 34:193-208

Skamarocius v. State, 731 P.2d 63 (Alaska App. 1987)

Smith SM, Vela E: Environmental context-dependent eyewitness recognition. Applied Cognitive Psychology 1992; 6:2:125-139

Smith VL, Ellsworth PC: The social psychology of eyewitness accuracy: misleading questions and communicator expertise. Journal of Applied Psychology 1987; 72:294-300

Snyder M: When belief creates reality? in Advances in Experimental Social Psychology (Vol. 18). Edited by Berkowitz L. Orlando, Academic Press, 1984; 247-305

Sobel NR: Eyewitness Identification: Legal and Practical Problems. New York, Clark & Boardman, 1972

Sobel NR: Eyewitness Identification: Legal and Practical Problems. (Second Edition). New York, Clark & Boardman, 1985

Sporer SL, Penrod SD, Read JD, Cutler BL: Choosing, confidence and accuracy: a meta-analysis of the confidence-accuracy relation in eyewitness identification studies. Psychological Bulletin 1995; 118:315-327

Sporer SL: Decision times and eyewitness identification accuracy in simultaneous and sequential lineups, in Adult Eyewitness Testimony: Current Trends and Developments. Edited by Ross DF, Read JD, Toglia MP. New York, Cambridge University Press, 1994

Sporer SL: Eyewitness identification accuracy, confidence, and decision times in simultaneous and sequential lineups. Journal of Applied Psychology 1993; 78:1:22-33

Sporer SL: Person descriptions in an archival analysis of criminal cases. Unpublished manuscript, University of Marburg, Germany, 1992

Sporer SL: Post-dicting eyewitness accuracy: confidence, decision-times and person descriptions of choosers and non-choosers. European Journal of Social Psychology 1992; 22:157-180

State of Kansas v. Warren, 635 P.2d 1236 (1981)

State v. Buell, 22 Ohio St.3d 124, 489 N.E.2d 795, cert. denied, 479 United States 871, 107 S. Ct. 240, 93 L.Ed.2d 165 (1986)

State v. Chapple, 135 Ariz. 281, 660 P.2d 1208 (1983)

State v. Malarney, 18 Fla. L. Week. D906 (1993)

State v. Moon, 45 Wash. App. 692, 726 P.2d 1263 (1986)

Stern LD, Dunning D: Distinguishing accurate from inaccurate eyewitness identifications: a reality monitoring approach, in Adult Eyewitness Testimony: Current Trends and Developments. Edited by Ross DF, Read JD, Toglia MP. New York, Cambridge University Press, 1994

Teitelbaum S, Geiselman, RE: Observer mood and cross-racial recognition of faces. Journal of Cross-Cultural Psychology, in press, 1996

Terry RL: Effects of facial transformations on accuracy of recognition. Journal of Social Psychology 1994; 134:483-492

Thucydides: 411 B.C. History of the Peloponnesian War, translation of 1628 by Thomas Hobbes; republished by University of Michigan Press, Ann Arbor, 2 vols., 1959

Tickner AH, Poulton EC: Watching for people and actions. Ergonomics 1975; 18:35-51

Tollestrup PA, Turtle JW, Yuille JC: Actual victims and witnesses to robbery and fraud: an archival analysis, in Adult Eyewitness Testimony: Current Trends and Developments. Edited by Ross DF, Read JD, Toglia MP. New York, Cambridge University Press, 1994

Tooley V, Brigham JC, Maass A, Bothwell RK: Facial recognition: weapon effect and attentional focus. Journal of Applied Social Psychology 1987; 17:845-849

Treadway M, McCloskey M: Site unseen: distortions of the Allport and Postman rumor study in the eyewitness testimony literature. Law & Human Behavior 1987; 11:19-25

Treadway M, McCloskey M: Effects of racial stereotypes on eyewitness performance: implications of the real and the rumored Allport and Postman studies. Applied Cognitive Psychology 1989; 3:53-63

Tremper CR: Sanguinity and disillusionment where law meets social science. Law & Human Behavior 1987; 11:4:267-276

Underwager R, Wakefield H: A paradigm shift for expert witnesses. Issues in Child Abuse Accusations 1993; 5:156-167

U.S. v. Amaral, 488 F.d2 1148 (9th Cir., 1973)

U.S. v. Archibald, 734 F.2d 938, 942 (2d Cir., 1984)

U.S. v. Ash, 413 United States 300 (1973)

U.S. v. Brown, 540 F.2d 1048 (10th Cir., 1976)

U.S. v. Collins, 395 F.Supp. 629 (M.D. Pa., 1975)

U.S. v. Downing, 753 F.2d (3rd Cir., 1985)

U.S. v. Jackson, No. 16158-74 (Super. Ct. D.C., 1975)

U.S. v. Poole, 794, F.2d 462, 468 (1986)

U.S. v. Rincon, 1994 WL 265047 (9th Cir., 1994); 93 Daily Journal D.A.R. 1309. Fed. R. App. P. 34

U.S. v. Smith, 736 F.2d 1103 (6th Cir., 1984)

U.S. v. Stevens, 935 F.2d 1380, 1400-01 (3rd Cir., 1991)

U.S. v. Telfaire, 469 F.2d 552 (DC Cir., 1972)

U.S. v. Wade, 388 U.S. 218, 18 L Ed 1149, 87 S Ct 1926 (1967)

Van Wallendael LR, Surace A, Parsons DH, Brown M: Earwitness voice recognition. Applied Cognitive Psychology 1994; 8:661-677

Visher CA: Juror decision making: the importance of evidence. Law and Human Behavior 1987; 11:1-17

Wagenaar WA: Comparison of one-person and many-person lineups: a warning against unsafe practices. Unpublished manuscript, Leiden University, Leiden, The Netherlands, 1992

Wall PM: Eyewitness Identification of Criminal Cases. Springfield, IL, Charles C. Thomas, 1965

Weingardt KR, Toland HK, Loftus EF: Reports of suggested memories: do people truly believe them? in Adult Eyewitness Testimony: Current Trends and Developments. Edited by Ross DF, Read JD, Toglia MP. New York, Cambridge University Press, 1994

Wells GL, Hryciw B: Memory for faces: encoding and retrieval operations. Memory & Cognition 1984; 12:338-344

Wells GL, Leippe MR, Olstrom TM: Guidelines for empirically assessing the fairness of a lineup. Law and Human Behavior 1979; 3:285-293

Wells GL, Leippe MR, Ostrom TM: Guidelines for empirically assessing the fairness of a lineup. Law and Human Behavior 1979; 3:285-293.

Wells GL, Leippe MR: How do triers of fact infer the accuracy of eyewitness identification? Using memory for peripheral detail can be misleading. Journal of Applied Psychology 1981; 66:682-687

Wells GL, Lindsay RC, Tousignant JP: Effects of expert psychological advice on human performance in judging the validity of eyewitness testimony. Law & Human Behavior 1980; 4:4:275-285

Wells GL, Lindsay RCL, Ferguson T: Accuracy, confidence and juror perception in eyewitness identification. Journal of Applied Psychology 1979; 64:440-448

Wells GL, Seelau EP, Rydell SM, Luus CAE: Recommendations for properly conducted lineup identification tasks, in Adult Eyewitness Testimony: Current Trends and Developments. Edited by Ross DF, Read JD, Toglia MP. New York, Cambridge University Press, 1994

Wells GL, Turtle JW: Eyewitness identification: the importance of lineup models. Psychological Bulletin 1986; 99:320-329

Wells GL, Turtule JW: Eyewitness identification: the importance of lineup models. Psychological Bulletin 1986; 88:776-784

Wells GL, Wright EF: Unpublished data. University of Alberta, cited in Wells GL: Expert psychological testimony. Law and Human Behavior 1983; 12:83-96

Wells GL: A re-analysis of the expert testimony issue, in Eyewitness Testimony: Psychological Perspectives. Edited by Wells GL, Loftus EF. New York, Cambridge University Press, 1984

Wells GL: Applied eyewitness testimony research: system variables and estimator variables. Journal of Personality and Social Psychology 1978; 36:1546-1557

Wells GL: Eyewitness Identification: A System Handbook. Toronto, Carswell, 1988

Wells GL: How adequate is human intuition for judging eyewitness testimony? in Eyewitness Testimony: Psychological Perspectives. Edited by Wells GL, Loftus EF. New York, Cambridge University Press, 1984; 256-272

Wells GL: The psychology of lineup identifications. Journal of Applied Social Psychology 1984; 14:89-103

Wells GL: Verbal descriptions of faces from memory: are they diagnostic of identification accuracy? Journal of Applied Psychology 1985; 70:619-626

Wells GL: What do we know about eyewitness identification? American Psychologist 1993; 48:553-571

Wells WP, Cutler BL: The right to counsel at videotaped lineups: an emerging dilemma. Connecticut Law Review 1990; 22:373-395

Whipple GM: The obtaining of information: psychology of observation and report. Psychological Bulletin 1918; 15:217-248

Whiteley BB, Greenberg MS: The role of eyewitness confidence in juror perceptions of credibility. Journal of Applied Social Psychology 1986; 16:387-409

Whittlesea L: Illusions of familiarity. Journal of Experimental Psychology: Human Learning and Memory 1993; 19:1235-1253

Wigmore JH: Professor Munsterberg and the psychology of testimony: being the trial of Cokestone v. Munsterberg. Illinois Law Review 1909; 3-399-345

Williams KD, Loftus EF, Deffenbacher KA: Eyewitness evidence and testimony, in Handbook of Psychology and Law. Edited by Kagehiro KK, Laufer WS. New York, Springer-Verlag, 1992

Woocher FD: Legal principles governing expert testimony by experimental psychologists. Law and Human Behavior 1986; 10:47-62

Woodhead MM, Baddeley AD, Simmonds DC: On training people to recognize faces. Ergonomics 1979; 22:333-343

Wrightsman LS, Neitzel MT, Fortune WH: Psychology and the Legal System. (Third Edition). Pacific Grove, CA, Brooks-Cole, 1993

Yarmey AD, Jones HPT: Is the psychology of eyewitness identification a matter of common sense? in Evaluating Witness Evidence: Recent Psychological Research and New Perspectives. Lloyd-Bostock S, Clifford BR. Chichester, UK, Wiley, 1983; 13-40

Yarmey AD, Kent J: Eyewitness identification by elderly and young adults. Law and Human Behavior 1980; 4:359-371

Yarmey AD, Kent J: Eyewitness identification by elderly and young adults. Law and Human Behavior 1980; 4:359-371

Yarmey AD, Yarmey AL, Yarmey MJ: Face and voice identifications in showups and lineups. Applied Cognitive Psychology 1994; 8:453-464

Yarmey AD, Yarmey AL: Relaxation-hypnotic enhanced memory and photographic lineup identification. Expert Evidence 1993; 2:115-119

Yarmey AD: Adult age and gender differences in eyewitness recall in field settings. Journal of Applied Social Psychology 1993; 23:1921-1932

Yarmey AD: Age as a factor in eyewitness memory, in Eyewitness Testimony: Psychological Perspectives. Edited by Wells GL, Loftus EL. 1984; 142-154

Yarmey AD: Earwitness evidence: memory for a perpetrator's voice, in Adult Eyewitness Testimony: Current Trends and Developments. Edited by Ross DF, Read JD, Toglia MP. New York, Cambridge University Press, 1994

Yarmey AD: Perceived expertness and credibility of police officers as eyewitnesses. Canadian Police Journal 1986; 10:31-52

Yarmey AD: The Psychology of Eyewitness Testimony. New York, Free Press, 1979

Yarmey DA, Matthys E: Voice identification of an abductor. Applied Cognitive Psychology 1992; 6:5:367-377

Yu CJ, Geiselman RE: Effects of constructing Identi-kit composites on photospread identification performance. Criminal Justice and Behavior 1993; 20:3:280-292

Yuille JC, Cutshall JL: A case study of eyewitness memory for a crime. Journal of Applied Psychology 1986; 71:291-301

Yuille JC, Davies G, Gibling F, Marxsen D, et al.: Eyewitness memory of police trainees for realistic role plays. Journal of Applied Psychology 1994; 79:931-936

Yuille JC, Tollestrup PA: Some effects of alcohol on eyewitness memory. Journal of Applied Psychology 1990; 75:268-273

Yuille JC: Research and teaching with the police: a Canadian example. International Review of Applied Psychology 1984; 33:5-24

Yuille JC: We must study forensic eyewitnesses to know about them. American Psychologist 1993; 48:572-573

Yuille JC: We must study forensic eyewitnesses to know about them. American Psychologist 1993; 48: 572-573

Zanni GR, Offermann JT: Eyewitness testimony: an exploration of question wording upon recall as a function of neuroticism. Perceptual and Motor Skills 1978; 46:459-482

Zaragoza MS, Lane L: Some misattributions and the suggestibility of eyewitness memory. Journal of Experimental Psychology: Learning, Memory, & Cognition 1994; 20:934-945